Life Stories

PAULA GILLILAND

ISBN 978-1-0980-5595-0 (paperback)
ISBN 978-1-0980-5897-5 (hardcover)
ISBN 978-1-0980-5596-7 (digital)

Copyright © 2020 by Paula Gilliland

All rights reserved. No part of this publication may be reproduced, distributed, or transmitted in any form or by any means, including photocopying, recording, or other electronic or mechanical methods without the prior written permission of the publisher. For permission requests, solicit the publisher via the address below.

Christian Faith Publishing, Inc.
832 Park Avenue
Meadville, PA 16335
www.christianfaithpublishing.com

Printed in the United States of America

Stories of the Past

Yes!

You really need to read this whole page.

I used to make up stories; some of them were to help someone fall sleep. I made up other stories also, but some of these are me just rambling on about things. So enjoy reading—I had fun writing these!

Some of the following stories are true. Can you guess which ones are true? Can you guess whom they are about? You have to know my family to do that. You have to remember how bad my rememberer is, so some of the stories may be a little different from what really happened. Please don't look for the grammar and punctuation mistakes (I think I got the spelling part right). It has been a long time since I had an English lesson; that is where you learned that kind of stuff when I went to school. Also, some time has passed since I wrote this, so some things may have changed.

All but one of these stories were written by Paula Gilliland, also known as Mom and Nana. The other story was found in a notebook tucked away in a closet. The story was written by Donald Gilliland, also known as Dad and Papaw. As you read it, you will know which one.

I didn't know that there would be so many stories and rambling on—hope you don't get bored. I hope you will remember to have fun and enjoy your life. Life is a gift. Make the most of it. It is okay to play, pretend, and you can even color, no matter what your age is. I love all of my family. I hope and pray you know that and don't forget it. Thank you for a great time.

A Frog

Some people like dogs, some cats, some horses, some birds, some fish—that is, to watch not eat—some turtles, some butterflies. There are so many things people could like. I don't have the space or time to name them all, and I don't think you would want to read it. But I will tell you of one person that likes a frog. This isn't just any ole frog; it is Kermit the Frog. I don't know how or where it all started or where she finds the things she has.

One time she found a pattern for Kermit on a Christmas stocking. She then asked her mother-in-law if she would make it for her. Her mother-in-law said she would try. So that year for Christmas, there was a Kermit the Frog on a stocking wrapped and put under the tree. When the gift was opened, I don't think anyone could have been more pleased at what they saw than she was.

So for many more years after that, there was some kind of Kermit the Frog item wrapped and put under the tree. There have been ornaments, sunglasses, a blanket, purses, drinking glasses, a cookie jar, and a board game—and that is just to name a few things I know of. I think that at one time she even had her husband paint their toaster to look like Kermit. I also know she had or has Kermit pajamas and a hat that looks like Kermit the Frog.

She keeps some of her items on display in her curio cabinet for all to see. You know there is only so much space in a home to put stuff. I don't know if all of this is because she likes green or Kermit. I do know of at least one time she had green hair. We all have silly things we like to collect and do. Just think about it. I know I have several.

A Little Girl and a Flagpole

One summer day, there was a little girl visiting her grandparents. She went out to play in the front yard; Nana could keep an eye on her from a window. There was a flagpole in the yard. When the girl saw the flagpole, she got excited. She thought she could climb it like a lumberjack climbs a tree; she had seen that on TV. She untied her shoes and tied the strings around the flagpole. Her shirt had a tie string also. You guessed it. So she tied it around the flagpole. Nana came out to check on her because she heard her hollering for help. Nana had seen her there and knew she wasn't in too much trouble.

It hadn't worked. She couldn't climb the flagpole like a lumberjack climbs a tree; she was stuck. Bad ole flagpole for not letting her climb it or letting her go. She couldn't untie her knots; she was stuck. So Nana untied her and let her loose from the flagpole. You see, Nana had been a champion knot tier when she was growing up, so she knew how to untie knots. And the little girl never tied herself to anything again—that is, trying to climb it like a lumberjack climbs a tree. So don't try to do everything you see on TV or videos; it isn't always possible to do. You may also get hurt or in trouble, and you may not have someone nearby you can call for help.

There is someone waiting to help you. All you have to do is ask. God is there. We may not be able to see Him physically, but He is there waiting to help. We just have to ask.

A Special Little Girl

Once upon a time, there was a little girl who didn't think she was very special at all. She thought no one liked her. Everyone else thought she was special in some way, but they didn't tell her. One cold winter day while she was at school, the teacher had a problem. Her problem was, she had little fuzz balls all over her sweater. They looked like little cotton balls. The teacher tried to pick them off but couldn't get any of them to come off.

One of the boys in her class said, "Let me try," and so she did. He pulled and pulled but couldn't get any of the balls to come off. One of the little girls also tried, but she couldn't get any off either. All the kids in the class except the one little girl took a turn trying to get the balls off the teacher's sweater. But no one had any luck; none of them could get any of the balls off. The teacher was sad. She thought she would have to get rid of the sweater. This made her sad; the sweater was her favorite.

So the last little girl tried to pull the balls off, and guess what—the balls started coming off the sweater, one at a time, as she pulled on it. Oh, the teacher was so happy. Her sweater was like new again. She didn't have to get rid of it after all. And so you see, the little girl who thought she was not special at all was very special because she was the only one that could pull the little cotton balls off the teacher's sweater.

We all are special in some way. We each have to find in what way we are special and then use our special talent to help others. You may not know what your special talent is. Others may be able to tell you, or there are tests out there that can help you find out.

We all have something special about us; we just need to try and find out what it is.

A Wife and Mother

Being a wife and mother is very rewarding. It has its drawbacks. When the wife part started, it was two people living in an apartment; that was okay. Then we moved to a trailer. That was even better as we had more space. Along came the mother part. There goes all the extra space we had. Our baby was sweet, but she had a lot of stuff. There was a swing; it stayed in the living room. There was a carrier called a pumpkin seat. It was a kind of car seat; you didn't buckle it in. It was very light, so it went back and forth from house to car.

The diapers were cloth, so there was a lot of them. There was a diaper pail to put the wet and dirty ones in till time to wash came. Washdays were different then. After the washing was done, then came the drying. The wet things were put in a basket and taken outside to be hung on a line to dry. After they were dry, you took them down and took them inside to be folded and put away.

Of course, the older the babies get, the more stuff they have. The toys are larger, tricycles, and then bicycles come along. And their clothes are bigger, so they take up more space.

And when a second child comes along, this starts all over again. And then if you have more, it just goes on and on.

And don't forget the husband and the house. There is always something to do. The house needs to be cleaned or straightened. Then there are the dishes, laundry, cooking, and sometimes there may be ironing and sewing to do. Beds to be made, toys to be picked up, dusting to be done. You think it will better after the kids are grown and moved out of the house.

There is also the grocery and clothes shopping for the family. You have to know what to buy so you don't run out. Ketchup and peanut butter are two of the main items that were important items when my kids were little. You have to be a good shopper. There was one time we only had $32 to spend on groceries for a family of four, and that was for two weeks.

Well, I can tell you that there is a lot of that work does not go away with the kids. The wash remains along with cooking, dishes, cleaning, straightening, and taking care of your man.

I started my trip down this road at the age of eighteen. I call it a trip because it has been a real journey. I did not mention all the moves. All the packing and then the house hunting. And when you do find a place to make a home, the unpacking. The unpacking is not that hard but trying to figure out what goes where.

The wife part is not easy either. Having a husband to take care of and worry about when his job takes him away. Not knowing where he is or when he will be back. Some husbands have jobs that put their life in danger. I was not allowed to know if this was happening. So every time, that thought was there. And with the roads the way they are today and the crazy drivers out there, the thought is still there every time he goes out by himself. In some places, it's not even safe to be out in your own yard.

That is where it is important to find the right house to make it your home. The right house is more than just a house: it becomes a home. A place you want to be and a place you feel safe. A place you don't mind spending a lot of time taking care of.

Taking care of—there is more to take care of than the home. There are the kids and husband to take care of when they got sick, no matter how you feel, or hurt knees, elbows or other parts. And good moms even try to doctor the sick and hurt animals the kids bring to her. There could be a time the dad is away, so the mom gets to fix a flat bike tire. I had no idea how to fix it, so I wrapped the tube with brown moving tape to patch the hole. I also learned to rewire a lamp, change a tire on the car, and I know that are other things I learned.

And after the grandkids start to come along, it may start all over. They may not be around all the time, but they may have things they leave with you, if they live close. There may be little notes they leave you or mail to you that you keep. And don't forget the pictures that they make for you. These can be put away along with the pictures and papers their parents did. The fridge can only hold so many notes and pictures.

Then don't forget all the pictures that were taken over all those years that had to be put into photo albums. That is, if you find the time to put them in albums. They may all be waiting in a box somewhere for you to get the time to put them in albums or to divide up among the kids and maybe the grandkids.

But after saying all this, let me tell you, I would do it all over again if there was a rewind button for my life. It has not always been easy, but whoever said being a wife and mother was? It has been a bed of roses, and you have to remember that roses have thorns. There are good and bad times in life. If there was no bad in life, then the good would not seem so good. Forget the bad, treasure the good. Make memories to treasure.

Amazing Dogs

One summer morning after a breakfast of all kinds of doughnuts, a family decided to go to a flea market. The family was visiting with some family members. They had even taken the dog with them. They put the leftover doughnuts back in their wax-covered paper bag. There was about two dozen left; they all fit in two bags, safely put in the center of the kitchen table where the dog could not get them. Or so they thought. Everyone got ready, and off they all went for a fun day—that's all except for the dog. He was left in the house. Hours later when they arrived back home, they weren't met at the door by the dog as usual. Instead, he was lying on the living room floor and only raised his head and moaned when they came in.

After a while, someone asked where the doughnuts had been put. The answer was, they had been left on the table. But they were not there. No doughnuts, no bags, they could not be found anywhere. The only thing that could have happened to them was that the dog got them and ate them bags and all. Maybe that is the reason he didn't meet them when they arrived; he only raised his head and moaned. The dog proved he liked chocolate.

Sometime later, the same family had moved and had a different dog. This dog was a girl and had been a drop-off dog. That's were someone just dumps a dog by the side of the road. The family took her and had her checked out by a vet. The vet guessed her age to be four months. The family took her in and raised her. They grew to love her. And the next part will show why and that she must have loved them also.

The mom of the family was out hanging clothes on the clothesline one day. The dog got in front of her and would not move. The dad came to see what the problem was and why this was happening. On the ground, a few feet away from the dog was a copperhead. The dog was protecting the mom from the snake. She probably saved the mom's life.

Several years later, late one night, the dad was having trouble sleeping. He got up and went outside, taking the same dog with him. As he was walking to the pool to take a dip, the dog stopped right in front of him. The dog would not move. The dad couldn't get around the dog, so he went and turned on the light to see what the matter was. There, on the ground in front of the dog, was another copperhead. The dog had saved the dad's life also.

The family loved the dog so much they kept her and took care of her till she passed away of old age. She was seventeen years old at that time. She has never been forgotten. Her collar hangs from the rear-view mirror of the dad's truck and has for years and will for many more to come.

Angels in Disguise I

A mother and her two small children were to take their first plane ride followed by a bus ride. None of them had ever traveled that far or by those modes of transportation before. On the small plane, there was a small table with two seats facing the table on each side. The mother had two tickets; that meant that the three of them and a diaper bag had to share the two seats.

Across the table were two other people. No spreading out; the plane was full. They were all strangers; they didn't know anything about one another. The mom and the young man across the table got to talking to each other. He asked if it was her first time traveling and where she and the kids were going. She looked nervous and scared. He told her he took this flight all the time, and he would help her when they landed, if it was okay. She agreed and was very thankful.

When they landed in Boston, Massachusetts, he helped her out of the airport. She had never been to such a big place before. They then shared a cab to the bus station. Once there, he told her to stay put; he would get the bus tickets and be right back. He told her not to let anyone take her luggage anywhere. He said that was a way to lose your belongings. She put the suitcase between her feet and held on to the kids. She stayed put till he came back.

When he got back, he rushed them off to a bus. He had bought the only ticket left for her and the kids. The bus was about to leave. They had to hurry to catch it. He wouldn't even let her pay him back for the ticket. What a gentleman. The bus ride was over an hour long, but it didn't seem to be that long. All the people around the mother and her kids were very nice. Some of them offered to hold the kids so they weren't all cramped up in the one seat. Remember the bus was full; no spreading out here either.

You know that there are angels out there that help people. Some people don't even realize who is helping them until later. They arrived safely at the bus station, where a big hug and lots of kisses awaited them. They were actually moving there to be with the kid's dad and the lady's husband. The first of many moves to be made by the family. And they don't believe it was the only time they were helped by an angel or angels. What has happened in your life that cannot be explained?

Age

There's a saying, "You are as old as you feel." I don't know about that. Sometimes one can feel really old, and then sometimes one can feel very young and foolish. There are the times when a couple might go to the lake to fish, or that is what some people call it. One person may fish, and the other one may just sit and enjoy the day. There is so much to look at. Take the time to look at all of creation. One could try to list it all, but there is too much. There is also strolling or walking along the edge of the water. You could also pick up rocks and shells. Just make sure the shells are empty if you are going to keep them in the house.

Oh, but don't get carried away with collecting the rocks. It's easy to do, just walking along making piles of rocks to carry back to your vehicle. You know rocks do get heavy while carrying all of them to your vehicle. If you find a lot, it may take more than one trip. You may think you are young enough to do it, but your body may tell you that you are not. Maybe not then; it could wait to tell you later.

There are memories that can remind you how old you are also: when you're talking to someone younger than you are about something that you did or watched when you were young, and they never heard of it. And then sometimes your body can just remind you how old you are for no reason at all. It may remind you with pain and/or stiffness. Or when you get up in the morning you, hurt all over for no reason other than being old. And some of you that are around young children will be told by them, "You are old." Also being around your grandchildren and trying to play with them the way you did with their parents—sometimes you can and sometimes you can't. And then there's the aftereffect on your aching body.

But there is an advantage to being older: there are senior discounts and sometimes going to the head of a line. Oh, but then there are times people will tell you that you are too old to do something, and of course, you must try to prove them wrong. That may not be the best choice to make. But you are old enough to make your own choices and mistakes, and no one can tell you what to do or not do. It wouldn't help anyway. You will do whatever you want, no matter what anyone says. You can make your own decisions. I know this from the past. Not only from others but myself. We are to learn from the past and not make the same mistakes. This doesn't always happen. We try to redo what we failed at before. Or we try to do what someone else may have failed at, thinking we can do it. This isn't always true.

Adults Adopting Adults

There was a couple. The dad went to Kroger a lot. He would always say "Howdy" and encourage everyone he met. There was this one young lady that worked in the bakery. He could tell she was bothered by something, but he didn't ask her what. He knew that if God wanted him to know, the young lady would tell him. Well, one day he went to Kroger as usual, but after he left the bakery section, he felt like someone was following him. He got around to the meat department and turned to see if it was just his imagination or if there really was someone there. It was the young lady from the bakery department. She came up to him and told him how important his encouraging her was. She had lost her dad about a year earlier and that he had been her encourager, and she missed and needed it. So she asked him if he could be her dad. He said yes. So from then on, she was family. She could come over anytime and was to call anytime she needed anything. She came over for sewing lessons from Mom, watch movies, have tea parties, and just talk, and she came for Christmas and brought her kids with her. As time went on, the parents had a lot of trouble with one of their other children. They both got to wondering if they were still good parents. They prayed for God to show them if they were or not. And He did.

One Sunday morning, they were at church as usual. A young couple they knew ask them if they could have a minute of their time. This was God's answer to them. The couple said they both grew up without good parents and asked if the couple would be their parents. The answer was yes, of course. But the dad said they had to take the good and the bad. He meant that if they did something wrong, he would let them know. And when they did something right, he would be there to pat them on the back and to encourage them on. The new family members then came over just to talk, watch movies, and she would come over for tea parties, no boys allowed. And they all enjoyed Christmas together after that day.

The family kept growing. A friend of the oldest daughter who had lost her mom and was missing her greatly met the parents. You guessed it, she asked the question, and they cried together, and then she and her husband became family too. The oldest daughter's friend and her husband adopted the couple as their parents. At Christmastime, they all get together, just one big happy family. And so the family continues to grow. No one knows how big the family will get, and they really don't care. There is enough love for all. God's love is the same; there is enough for everyone. Even if you don't know Him, He still loves you.

Angels in Disguise II

As a young man traveled to basic training, he had a layover in Philadelphia International Airport. He made his way to the USO. When he arrived, a woman greeted him. She told him her name was Marge. She offered him a bologna sandwich, chips, and a soda. As they got to talking, she told him why she was there. It was not just to help service men and women or to offer them something to eat. Being there made her feel a little closer to her husband. After being married only a few days, she saw him off to go fight in World War II. That was the last time she ever saw him. It helped her to be there and help others. The man was touched by her story. He never forgot her or her story.

When the same man and his wife went to their son's graduation from Coast Guard basic training, they all had a layover in Philadelphia International Airport. The man was wondering if Marge was still there in the USO serving sandwiches and sodas. They all went to see, and there she was—still serving some twenty years later. The man was surprised to see that she was still there and looked the same as he remembered her. He explained to her that she had served him before and how much it meant to see her still there serving. She again offered to make them a bologna sandwich and get them a soda.

Several weeks later, the man couldn't stop thinking about Marge. He got the address for the main office of the USO at the Philadelphia International Airport. He sat down and wrote them a letter all about his and then his family's experience with Marge. To his surprise, he received a letter back from them. But the biggest surprise was that no one named Marge ever worked there, and no one had worked there for more than three years; he must be mistaken. The man, his wife, and son all saw her. How could they all be mistaken? The family believes she must have been an angel in disguise.

The story has been told many times, and all who hear of the encounter agree. God's angels are all around. We never know when we are with one or one is with us.

Bay versus Ocean

This story begins with a couple taking their granddaughter on a trip with them to go see their youngest son. He was not at home with his family; they didn't live close by. He was away from his family for some schooling. His job required him to take this schooling. The trip took a couple days to get there. They had to travel from Tennessee to Virginia; they chose to drive so they could see everything on the way there. It was a job keeping a five-year-old entertained for the whole trip. Nana had filled a bag with all kinds of things to keep the girl busy; we will call her Abby. There were some of her favorite books to read or look at, a drawing pad, a dry-erase board, and a mirror. The mirror was because Abby liked looking at herself and making funny faces. Abby was told that they were going to Virginia. This was confusing to Abby because she knew a lady at her church named Virginia. Abby kept asking where Ms. Virginia was.

The day they arrived in Virginia, it was late. Abby couldn't wait to see the big water; that was what she called the bay and the ocean. Jim, the son and uncle, drove them to a bay. Abby was very excited to see it. She didn't want to leave it so they could go to the room Jim had gotten for them to stay in. They did get her to go, with the idea they would be going to see bigger water in the morning. In the morning, Abby kept bugging them to go to see the bigger water. After breakfast, they all went to the ocean. Abby was so amazed and a little bit scared of the waves. The waves almost knocked her down several times. One wave did knock her down and went over her—she loved it.

When she and her papaw were in the water, Abby stopped and said, "Isn't it amazing all that God has made?" This surprised her papaw. Such an amazing statement from a little girl. After a day at the beach and going around seeing all there was to see, they ate at a hot-dog place. It was called, Hot Dog King. There was a six-foot-tall hot dog you could stand by and have your picture taken, and Abby did. After a long day, they went back to their room to sleep.

In the morning, they didn't know what to do. Abby wanted to go back to what she called the big water. She didn't want to go to the bay. They don't know why she liked the ocean better, maybe because the ocean is so big or because it has big waves. Later, when the time came for Jim to go back to school, the visit with Jim had been just for a weekend because he was at a school. Not what some people would call a school. He had to go to a class for the Coast Guard. Monday morning came. Jim went off to class, and Abby and her grandparents left to head home to more adventures.

I guess if the bay and ocean did go against each other, the bay would be gobbled up by the ocean. Do you know how to tell the difference between the two? If you put your ear down to the ocean, you will hear a shell. If you don't get it, just ask you parents or grandparents to explain it. If they don't know, then I guess you are out of luck. It is an old joke, sort of.

Believe It or Not

My mother always had an answer for every question anyone ever asked her. Oh, the answer may not have fit the question, but she had an answer. There were two different answers she used a lot. The first was, "Cook it till it is done." The second answer was, "Fifty cents." As you can tell, these answers won't work all the time. I have noticed that I even use these answers sometimes, and so have my kids. If your kids ask you if you remember something, and you don't just tell, then, "Wrong, Momma, try again." But this can backfire on you too. If you ask them something, they may say, "Wrong, child, try another."

Doing the dishes with the kids can also be fun. If there are bottles with nipples to be washed, someone may be squirted with water from the nipple. I can remember several times having someone feed me the dishrag. Of course, I returned the act of feeding them the rag. Saying you have to go to the bathroom while doing the dishes may not help get you out of doing them. Some people just keep washing them and piling them in your sink.

I went outside one cold winter morning about seven thirty and made a big fire in the firepit. The whole neighborhood was filled with smoke. By the time nine thirty came around, I had warmed the outside up. You see, I like to make big fires. I even know how to get smoldering leaves to burn. You take and put some gasoline in a Ziploc sandwich bag and place it on top of the leaves, then back away. The smoldering leaves melt the bag, and the leaves take off. Sometimes they take off flying everywhere. I was told not to do that anymore; I may blow myself up. I was also told not to squirt lighter fluid on a burning fire or to throw gasoline on a fire. But I received a woodpile and a gallon of gasoline that year for my birthday. So what was I to do? I made a big fire. I think I have enough sense to stay back far enough. I have never been blown up or burnt yet.

Bets and Stories

There once was a couple who had been married for quite some time. So long that they both were in high school together and now were retired together. One evening when they had nothing to do—ha-ha—they decided to play some video games. The woman got the tablet and lay on the bed. A tablet is a small version of a laptop. The man sat at his desk with the computer. There they were together but separate playing their games; they did this for quite a while. The man got an idea. He made a bet with the woman. The bet was to see who could go the longest without playing any kind of video games or work any puzzles. The woman took the bet.

To help them pass the time during the day, they started playing cards or watching movies together. Well, one day the woman had nothing to do, or nothing she wanted to do. The man was busy doing something somewhere else, so the woman picked up the tablet, not to play games, but she started writing stories. So now you know why these stories were written. So enjoy yourself as you read. I think you will. I know I did. And as I go through them again and again, I still enjoy reading them.

The Blue Washrag

There once was a little girl who would only use a blue washrag. If her mom didn't give her a blue washrag to use at bath time, the little girl would throw a fit. One day at bath time, all the blue washrags were in the wash. The little girl fussed and fussed for a blue washrag. Her mom told her they were all dirty, but the little girl continued to fuss. Her mom gave the little girl a pink washrag; it did no good. The little girl fussed even louder. The mom left the room and closed the door behind her. After a little while, the mother noticed that the little girl was no longer fussing. Was she going to bathe without a blue washrag? The mom went to see. To the mom's surprise, her daughter was not in the tub. There was the pink washrag and a blue washrag. Where had her daughter gone? Where did the blue washrag come from? The mom would have seen her daughter if she got the washrag out of the laundry.

The house was searched; no daughter anywhere. Had it happened? Had the little girl somehow turned into a blue washrag? *Oh, what will I do?* the mother thought. *How can I get my daughter back?* The mom went into the bathroom and started to wash the pink washrag with the blue one. To the mother's surprise, the blue washrag slowly turned into her little girl. No one knows how a thing like that could happen, but the little girl didn't want to be a washrag again. So from then on, she used whatever color washrag she was given. The mom didn't want her daughter to be a washrag again either. It was made sure that the little girl was given a rainbow of different colors.

What color washrag do you use all the time? Do you fuss if your favorite-color rag is dirty? Does this story apply to dishrags also? What about towels?

Bows

There is a couple who have grown children. These children also have children. One of the younger couples have a beautiful little girl. The girl has beautiful long blonde hair. This is where the bows come in. She is always seen with a bow in her hair. The bows are of all sizes. They sit upon her head like a crown. Every time the grandparents see this little girl, she has a beautiful bow in her beautiful long blonde hair. Her hair is also very curly. As she grows up, she continues to wear bows in her hair. The grandmother thought she must have one that would match any outfit she had—pink ones, purple ones, blue ones, some were multiple colors, and there even has been a polka-dot one, maybe more than one.

Now these are not regular bows. These are bows the girl's mother makes for her. So they are special bows. It must have taken lots of time and love to make all those bows. Small ones, large ones, and some middle-size ones. Does anyone know just how many bows there have been over the years? Does anyone know if she still has all of them? Where do you keep that many bows? Is there a special way to keep them so they don't get smashed? I'm glad I don't have to count the number of bows or find a place to keep them.

Boys to Men

There was a couple that had three children. The oldest two had grown up and moved away. The youngest son of the family got a job far away from home. The reason for that is he couldn't find a job that he thought he could spend the rest of his life doing in the city they were living in. These are his words. While he was gone, he met a beautiful young woman. You guessed it, they fell in love and got married. But let's go back in time a little. When he called his parents to tell them about her, he told them that she had two sons living at home. I don't know if their response surprised him or not, but his parents told him they would take the grandchildren any way they could get them.

Okay, so they got married. The wedding was so sudden and so far away that the parents (and now grandparents) again didn't make it to the wedding. And so about six months later, the newlyweds came to visit so that the two families could meet. They all got together; they loved one another instantly. The boys have grown up to be fine young men. Believe it or not, they listened to their parents when they were young. I think they still do. Or at least they did last time I heard. They have grown up to be handsome, respectful men. The grandparents are proud to have them in the family. There were three boys to men in this story. I know that there isn't much in this story about boys or men. But I needed to tell you about the boys who became men. Can you figure out who the third boy was?

Bunnies

There once was a man who had two sons. But now he has four. But this story is only about two of them because the third and fourth sons weren't known of yet. This man and his sons liked to hunt. They hunted all kinds of animals. One day they got dressed and ready to go hunting. Now this was not a small task. There were extra layers of clothes to put on, ammo to gather up, and guns to get ready—and of course, get the boys together too. Oh, don't forget the drinks and snacks. Growing boys always need to eat and drink, or so they think. And then they all had to get into the truck with all their stuff and go. They went to a friend's land to hunt poor little bunnies. When they got there, they had to walk some to get to the spot where they had been told that they could get some rabbits for sure. As they hunted, they never saw any rabbits, or said they didn't because they missed them all. So they walked back to the truck and went home. They were all tired from all the hunting, walking, and looking for rabbits. Of course, Mom asked, "Where all the little bunnies?" They told her, "The poor little bunnies were still at home, with their families." They didn't shoot any. So they didn't have bunnies for supper.

At a later time in their lives, they did go out hunting and brought home some poor little bunnies for dinner. The youngest son recently brought three big bunnies home for his mother to cook. He and his wife hunted them down; they were found at the grocery store. I wonder if that is as much fun and work as going out to the fields to hunt them?

Butterflies

This is a story about my coming to like butterflies. Almost thirty years ago, my husband and I bought a house. The front porch had been enclosed to make a room. On the side facing the neighbors was a big plain square spot on the wall. I thought it needed something on it. One day at a yard sale, I found some twelve-inch-tall plastic butterflies, and I bought them for that wall. I liked the way it looked. I added more as time passed. I also bought different kinds of butterflies for inside the house.

My collection has expanded past plastic butterflies. I now have real butterflies displayed all around the house; there are also pictures and paintings. I have butterflies on my curtains and magnets on the fridge and stickers on the light-switch covers and some on the walls also. I gave a set of dishes with butterflies on them to my granddaughter. I have several different sets of butterfly dishes for myself. I also have a collection of fine china from England with butterflies in the pattern.

Someone once said that if all the butterflies in the house came to life, the house would fly away. The amount of butterflies in the house was around four hundred items. Besides all those items, I also have two china cabinets in the living room full, or shall I say overfull, of all different things with butterflies on them. Oh, and let's not forget the clothes and purses that have butterflies on them. I also have started a quilt with butterflies and have lots more material with butterflies to make something else with; I haven't figured out what to make yet.

Back to the real butterflies. I think they are amazing, the way God made so many different kinds and colors. There is a butterfly from Peru that is different colors on the top and underneath side. To watch a butterfly flutter around is also amazing to me. They look so graceful and dainty. Some people say they are a symbol of hope. To start out in life as a wormlike creature and then turn into a beautiful creation—a butterfly. Isn't that amazing? Isn't God amazing?

Car Problems?

Here are a few different kinds of car problems that have been known to happen. You get to choose if it is the car or the driver that caused the problem—or could it even be the problem?

On a cold windy night, the family car was borrowed by one of the children. It was supposed to be driven to work and then back home. She has said that work is the only place she would go. So her parents are sitting waiting for her to get home. It is past the time she should have been home. They wonder if she is okay. The phone rings. Is it her? Is she okay? Yes, yes. She then tells them why she is late. The car quit and wouldn't start. She tells them where she is so they can come see if dad can fix the car. She isn't in between work and home. She is over ten miles past home. This must be taking a new long way home. Dad gets bundled up and goes to see if he can get the car started. But no luck; it is broken. A tow truck needs to be called. This was before cell phones, so someone would have to go get a tow truck or find a phone and call one. Dad says it isn't gonna be him; he wasn't the one who wasn't where they were supposed to be. The daughter then informs him it's cold outside. He already knew this; he is out in it. So off she goes on foot to find a phone. After the car is towed home, the driver wants to be paid. He looks at his daughter and says, "Pay him." She asks why. He tells her that if she would have come home like she was supposed to, the car wouldn't have had to been towed.

Another problem is every time you go to use the car, it is almost out of gas. You know you just filled it the day before. You're sure someone is stealing the gas. Your spouse then reminds you that your son borrowed the car to drive to a friend's house. You know it's not that far; it wouldn't take that much gas to just go to a friend's house. Someone must be stealing the gas. Your spouse is sure that it is being driven out. You take and fill the car up again. You write down the mileage to prove it's not being driven that much. The same son borrows the car again to drive to a friend's house. In the morning, you check to see how much gas is in the car. Almost empty again—that darn thief. You check the mileage, and there is almost a two-hundred-mile difference. You ask your son where all he went. He says to a friend's house and then to another friend's house and around town a little bit before he took his friends home. You find out there isn't a thief stealing the gas. The gas is being driven out.

There was a young man who owned his first car, no more borrowing the family car. One day his dad noticed a small dent in the center of the front bumper. He asked his son how it happened. After a small pause, the son told him it happened when he had been leaving work one late night. He was tired and not paying attention to the truck in front of him. They were stopped at a stop sign, and his car kinda rolled forward into the truck's ball hitch. That is what caused the dent. The dad had seen a dent like that before. It was from when he pushed a shopping cart with his car just to see how fast a cart could go. The son admitted that was what happened to his car also. There had been a cart left in the parking lot when he got off. It was dark, and no one was around, so he tried to see how fast a cart would go. Like father, like son.

The same car smoked, but it wasn't from the exhaust. The car was being driven home one day. The parents of the driver were going for a walk, and here comes their son in his car. It stopped so the son and his parents could talk. As the dad was talking, he noticed smoke coming up between the driver's door and the seat. The car must be on fire. Or was it just the son trying to hide a cigarette from his parents?

Have you ever been told by anyone where they were going and then they didn't go there? There was one time a teenager told her parents that she was going bowling with some friends. After several hours had gone by, one of the fathers called, needing to get ahold of his daughter. The two fathers talked about the plans they had been told. Then one of them called the bowling alley where the girls were supposed to be. They weren't there and had never been there. The families started to worry that there was something wrong. Where were they? All the girls were going to be in trouble when they showed up, if they were all right. The girl driving the car took her friends home and then went home too. Her dad was waiting for her and wanting to know where she had been. The story he got was that one of the girls had a problem and needed to talk to someone about it. The girls decided that the bowling alley would be too noisy to talk, so they went somewhere else. They had been at a fast-food restaurant talking the whole time they were gone. They didn't think to call anyone and tell them the plans had changed.

Some car problems also happen to adults. A woman and her son went to clean out a house that the family owned and rented out. On the way home, the truck they were driving just up and quit and wouldn't start again. This happened a little before dark on a busy parkway. The mom got out and found something red to wave so she could get a driver's attention. The only thing that could be found was a small red jacket. She stood behind the truck and waved it at the oncoming traffic. Someone noticed and called the police station to send help. When a policeman arrived, he let them sit in the back seat of his car and wait for the tow truck. It was the first time either of them had been in the back seat of a police car. They had the truck towed to a nearby gas station. The mechanic on duty said he could fix the truck the next day. What to do? Who to call? It wasn't Ghostbusters. It wouldn't help to call the dad either; he was away doing some training. They were about an hour from home with no money. They couldn't stay in the gas station overnight. They called someone from the church where they went, and an hour later, someone came all that way to give them a ride home. The next day, the truck got fixed, and they went and got it.

One last story about an amazing tire job. One evening, the youngest child in a family asked to borrow the car. When he got home, he didn't go in the house right away. When he did go in, he went straight to his room without saying a word. The next day, he got up and walked to school as usual. Several hours later, he called home and asked if anyone was going to use the car or had used it.

His dad asked him why. The answer was shocking. The night before when he was out with the car, he hit a curb and knocked a chunk out of one of the tires. So when he got home, he had gone to the garage to get something to fix it. He had filled the spot with Bondo. Then he carefully painted it so no one could tell. He had gotten to thinking about it and didn't want anyone driving the car and getting hurt because of him. As punishment, he was given the choice of getting the tire replaced or getting the car washed or washing the car himself once a week for a month. He chose to wash the car or get it washed; he thought it would be cheaper than a tire.

Career Day

This is a day you can take teenage kids to work with you. This is so they can see what you do at work. They may even decide that is what they want to do or be when they grow up. It didn't work that way for at least one family I know. Let me tell you about that family. The family had three children. The dad worked, and the mom was a stay-at-home mom. When the oldest child became a teenager and career day was coming around, her dad asked if she wanted to go to work with him. She agreed because it meant no school for a day. The long-awaited day came. Time to get up and get ready for the day. It was going to be a long day for the daughter. The time to get up was even before the sun was up. The daughter didn't like that very much; she thought she would get to sleep longer. Up and off to work they went.

First was physical training, then shower and getting dressed and ready for the workday. There was a lot of paperwork and reports to do. Lunchtime came and was spent in the office; mom had sent some of leftovers from the night before. After that, there was an afternoon filled with meetings and more reports to get ready. Then the time came for everyone to go home, but the dad still had work to do. The two of them got home about 7:30 p.m. The daughter told her dad she didn't want to do what he did when she grew up. The days were too long and too much paperwork.

Then the next child's turn came. He also chose to go to work with his dad. The day was about the same as his sister's day had been: up early and home late, lunch in the office, and a ton of paper work. He also chose not to go into his dad's line of work.

The time came for the last child to choose if he would go to work with his dad or not. He had heard about his older sister's and brother's days at work with their dad. He thought he was tougher than the other two and could take it. Well, after his long, hard day at work with his dad, he decided not to follow in his father's footsteps.

The daughter stuck with her decision and didn't follow in the dad's footprints. The oldest son also stuck with his decision and didn't follow in his dad's footprints. The youngest son also didn't follow in his dad's footprints, sort of. He didn't join the army like his dad had; instead, he joined the Coast Guard.

Even though the kids didn't join the army, they did enjoy the army field days and Week of the Eagle. Those are days they got to go and see and do some of the things their dad did, things more exciting than paperwork. They once got to see a fake helicopter and tank. By fake, that means it looked real but was either a blown-up life-sized item or one made from cardboard that looked real. The reason for this is to fool the enemy. They also got to put on a harness and jump out of a thirty-four-foot tall tower. They were hooked to a cable that went from the tower to the ground with someone there to catch them. It was also a time to go through obstacle courses and avoid trip wires. There were a lot of other things to do; this is just a few. No reports to do.

Cars in the Hospital

There once was a boy who had to have his appendix taken out. Now this boy was a young little boy; he was only seven years old. I don't know what his appendix had against him. He was an active little boy, always playing with someone or something. He liked to play with Matchbox cars, zooming them all around anywhere and everywhere. After his operation, he had to stay in the hospital for a week. It was hard to get him to stay still for that long. During that week, he got in trouble with the nurses several times. The first time was when he and his roommate were zooming their cars off their bedside tables and crashing them into the door and walls, which made a lot of noise. They said they were trying to jump them from bed to bed and missed. The more noise they made, the more they liked it. They got in trouble for all the noise they were making—"Shh, you're in a hospital." But boys do make noise, no matter where they are.

Every day he had to have some antibiotics through his IV. He didn't like that. One day at about the time for them, he got the idea to hide up in the bedsprings. He was hiding from the nurses so he didn't have to get the medicine. It didn't work; they found him. I bet the nurses in the hospital were glad to see him go home. Not only because he was well but to have him out of their hair and back with his family again.

Chalk Body Outlines

You may have seen these on a police show. Most of the time, they are where a dead body had been lying. I don't know if it is really a chalk or paint outline. A dead body isn't the reason for them everywhere. You see, some children like to be outlined. Let me explain.

There is one little girl who likes to lie on her grandparents' driveway and have her Nana trace around her. On the days that this happens, there is usually more than one chalk body outline when they are done. There are usually some flowers and maybe even a rainbow to go with them. The grandparents don't mind, and don't care what other people may think about it. The idea is to have fun and enjoy being with each other.

Now to change it a little. As the granddaughter has grown, the drawings have changed. No more body outlines. They have been replaced with tic-tac-toe games; the flowers and rainbows still are drawn. And at this time, no one knows what will be drawn the next time or at any time in the future. Or will there be any more drawings? The chalk is there and ready to be used again.

Let's go way back in time to wherever the little girl's older sister was young. The drawing of flowers was done by her. Somehow a crayon got into the chalk container. No one noticed. A flower was drawn and colored in. After it had rained several days later, someone noticed that some of the flowers hadn't been washed away. That is when the crayon was discovered and removed from the chalk container. The flowers parts lasted several weeks.

The grandparents have been very careful not to let that happen again.

Clothes

I have noticed that over the years of my life, clothes have changed. I will start with shoes: They have had become much more colorful; they aren't just black and white. The ones that were popular in years past have gone out of style and come back into style again. And what has happened to socks? They used to match. That meant they looked the same. Now socks are sold in packs where no two socks are the same. The color is different, and the design or pattern is different. Sometimes they are even different lengths. Also, females wore their bras under their shirt, and it was not the only item worn as a covering on the upper torso at any time. You ladies know what I mean. Oh, I will get to the guys a little later.

Shirts were also different: they covered the whole top area of the body up to the base of the neck and came down below the belly button at least, and that's where they stayed. They were not so short or low cut that they barely covered anything. And if the top and bottom clothing items worn both had flowers or stripes, they had to match. And as far as pants go, they were patched or thrown out if they were all ripped up and worn out. Also, when they got so tight a person could tell if the change in your pockets was heads or tails, you got rid of them. Pants also were not worn so tight that they looked like they were spray-painted on.

What about dresses and shorts, you ask? Well, they both came down to about knee-length. Neither were so short that underwear or butt was hanging out, and they weren't all ripped up or tight either. And what was called tights, an underwear item, are now called leggings and worn as a clothing item. Don't wear so much perfume that it chokes everyone; a small amount goes a long way.

LIFE STORIES | 39

Okay, guys, your time has come. The same goes for your pants: if they are all ripped up and worn out, throw them out. And if your pants are so big, they won't stay up; they hang down, and your boxers or panties show—that was and is a no-no. That is when you get smaller pants or wear a belt (make sure the belt is tight enough to keep your pants up). Pants stayed at the waistline on both females and males. The shirts worn weren't all ripped up, especially at the armhole or neckhole. If you work, after work and you are smelly and dirty, take a shower and put on some clean clothes before you do anything else. Yes, they can be clothes that have been worn but not yet dirty. Girls like clean-smelling guys, but don't wear too much. You want girls to fall for you, not pass out.

People always dressed up nicely when they were going out in public. They had what they called good clothes and everyday clothes. And when you got up in the morning, you took your pajamas off and got dressed—that's if you weren't sick and going to stay in bed all day. If you didn't get your clothes very dirty, you put them somewhere, not in the wash or on the floor but somewhere so you could find them to wear them again.

And as far swimsuits, they weren't skin-tight and smaller than a person's underwear. That means that they could have been someone's underwear. No body parts hung out the bottom, and nothing was popping out of the top. This is extra. When you went to the beach, all suits stayed on.

Children didn't get any say in what clothes or shoes were bought for them; the parents picked it all out. There was no concern about the name on the tag or if shoes had some famous sports guy's name on them. The purpose of clothes was to cover and keep a body warm. Shoes had the same purpose to cover and protect, not so tall you might fall over in them. Like I said, nobody cared about name brands. I don't even know if there were none brands.

This is just something extra to think about. Children also didn't argue with their parents about wearing a coat, gloves, a hat, or rubber rain boots if the weather called for it. Children didn't argue with their parents about anything. A child, no matter what age, didn't back talk or be disrespectful to any adult.

Cowboy Night

There was a middle-aged couple who on Friday nights would have what they called *cowboy night*. The name came from their childhoods. On Friday nights, both of their families would have bologna sandwiches and chips and drink sodas while they watched cowboy shows or movies on TV. This was kind of strange that both families did it because the families didn't know each other. However, they did live in the same small town. I guess that was something every family might have done way back then. And so the couple wanted to carry on the tradition with their family, hoping their children would carry it on too. They changed it a little bit. They would invite family and friends to come over and watch cowboys. This time, they were on DVD because there weren't any good ones on TV anymore. They also ate bologna sandwiches and chips and drank sodas. Sometimes they got wild and changed the menu or added to it.

Well, on with the story. There was this one couple that came over several times. Each time they came, they ate, and then one of them would hunt out the fuzzy pink blanket and cuddle up with it on the couch. And before you knew it, she was asleep; she missed out on watching cowboys. I don't think she really cared, and it didn't bother anyone else that I was told about. She also would go to the garage and get sodas in glass bottles for her husband and herself. There was a soda machine in the garage. The couple that hosted the cowboy nights thought it was great that she was so comfortable in their home she would do that. She was really family, and so was—or shall I say *is*—her husband.

Dating and Marriage

Dating before I ever started dating, my father told me if a boy wants to date me, he would have to come to the door and knock, not just sit in the driveway and honk. That knocking was the respectable thing to do.

I met someone, and here were the rules: I had limits on how much I could see the boy. It was two school nights, but only 'til 10:00 p.m., and then on Saturday, but not until after noon. The reason was because of the cleaning I had to do. The time I had to be home Saturday nights varied on what we were going to be doing or where we were going. On Sunday, he could come out and either go to church with me or take me to church. You see, we went to different churches. Of course, I had to be home by 10:00 p.m. You know they said it was because of school, but it didn't change in the summertime.

A note to dating couples (this goes for married couples also): doing something special for the other one doesn't stop when you get married. They should still be worth the effort. You know what I mean. Guys, if you gave her flowers, continue, even if you have to go and pick them somewhere. Just ask first if it's not your own yard. If you opened doors for her, go ahead and keep doing it. And, gals, if you got all fancied up and smelling good, don't stop just because you already got him. I don't know how it is now, but when I was dating, it was the guys who paid for everything. Gals, don't go too far with that. If the plan is to marry, he needs to save up. Guys, there are things that can be done that are not expensive and you both will enjoy. Here are a few: go for a picnic, go to a park and just sit and talk, cook something together for one of the families or a friend, take her swimming, and there are many more. Use your imagination.

Remember that dating isn't just for fun, but it still can be fun. The purpose for dating is to find the person you want to spend the rest of your life with and then to marry them. Marriage—oh, the happy bliss—well, not all the time. I was told that in marriage, if each gives 110 percent, it will be a good marriage. Okay, you math experts, figure that out. What it really means is to give it your all. Put in that extra effort on all you do. Do the big and small things that please the other one.

Ladies, if there's a food your husband likes and you don't, cook it anyway just for him. Give him a back rub, even if his back is okay. Keep his nails trimmed, both hands and feet. If he comes home with tired, hurting feet, give him a foot massage. It might or would be better after a shower or bath. When your man comes home from work, have a good meal ready or almost ready to be enjoyed by both of you together. Take the time to sit and talk with him. If he is the kind that needs to unwind or chill for a bit, let him do that. If he needs to sit and take a load off his mind, let him do that. I also know from personal experience that some husbands like being met at the door with a kiss.

Guys, you think that sounds good, just wait—your turn has come. Unless you are a millionaire, you have to provide the income for your now family. Yes, she may choose to work; that doesn't mean you can sit around and do nothing. Don't be a sponge and live off what she makes. Always be there when she needs a shoulder to cry on, even if you don't understand why she is crying. Just hold her and let her cry.

This part is for both of you: In marriage, there's no his-and-hers tasks or money. What is his is hers, and what is hers is his. Both can do dishes, laundry, cleaning, vacuuming, and that includes dusting. The yard and vehicle can be done by both; most men do it because they know how to the best. Always remember those wedding vows and stick with them. There is nothing you two can't make it through with the help of God. The kids can be taken care of by both; women usually do that because the men have to work. However, that doesn't mean that you guys can't give her a break and care for them sometimes. Feeding, bathing, and changing diapers also can be done by both parents.

Now the good part—yes, there should still be some romantic times. It could be as simple as a candlelight dinner at home or at a quaint little restaurant. Don't forget that just because you are married, the hugging and kissing have to stop, and don't forget to tell each other "I love you a lot" and tell them often. Show the other that they are still important to you. And don't forget to love the kids also, no matter what they may do or not do. The secret to a good marriage is no secret. The answer is to let God be in control. Then you *both* must work to keep it good. You both have to put the other person first. You both have to work to keep it happy. You both have to work to keep it together. If you really, really love God and each other, it's easier to do.

Deers, Bears, and Bugs

There once was a man and woman who had a baby. When the grandparents first saw her, they both said she was cute and so dear to them. The grandmother got an idea. She would get the granddaughter something every year for Christmas that was a deer or had a deer on it, and so she did.

Well, as time went on, another granddaughter was born in the family. Well, this time, the grandparents thought she was so cute they both wanted to give her a great big bear hug. So—you guessed it—she got a bear or something with a bear on it for Christmas every year.

Well, as more time passed, you guessed it. There was another granddaughter born. Well, with this one, the grandparents thought she was as cute as a bug. The grandmother got another idea: it was to get this granddaughter a bug or something with a bug on it every year for Christmas. Most years, it was a ladybug. The grandparents also had two grandsons. The grandparents didn't know the boys as babies, but I bet they both were handsome baby boys. They have grown up to be handsome men.

Don'ts

Do you remember as a child being told not to do something? Sometimes that made you want to do it that much more, didn't it? Or if you were told to do something, that made you not want to do it. Here are some examples of what should not be done. Please don't try them—oops.

Don't be in such a hurry to get somewhere that you don't make sure everyone is buckled up. Let me tell you why. There was a couple and their two kids. They were in a hurry to get somewhere (they didn't say where). Well, anyway, the parents thought it would be okay if the kids didn't buckle up; it wasn't that far. As the car turned left at a stop sign, the rear door flew open. The youngest child was falling out of the car, so the other child grabbed him, and they both feel out onto the road. Now you know this all happened in just seconds. The dad stopped the car and got out to see if the kids were okay. There was a car that came along and parked behind them, and they got out to check on the kids too. Of course, their mom got out also, but she was slower because there was going to be another child in a few months. Okay, okay, back to the kids, crying and lying in the road. Both were okay, just a few scrapes and scratches. The parents took them both to an emergency room to be checked out just to make sure.

Don't let your two youngest children, or any child or children, jump off the end of the couch onto a bean-bag chair. I heard of this happening firsthand. The oldest child of three was in her room playing. As I said, the two youngest were taking turns jumping off the arm of the couch. It was only about a foot to the bean-bag chair; mom didn't think anyone would be hurt. She told them to stop anyway as she went to the kitchen to do something. Oh, how wrong she was. The youngest child didn't get off the bag, so his older brother jumped on top of him. Well, heads bumped together. The oldest child split his head open just above the eyebrow. He didn't run to his mom. He ran into his older sister's room and put his head on the bed by her. She wasn't worried about him, just the fact he got blood on her sheets. Mom heard his crying and hunted him down. When she found him, which wasn't hard to do as it was a small house, she loaded them all into the car, and off they went to the emergency room. What about the youngest child? All he got was a bruise on his forehead. His brother, however, had to have stiches put in his head. They all three got over it quickly. Kids bounce back quick, but their heads don't bounce good.

Don't go to the beach on a warm breezy summer day, and if you do, don't lie out in the sun. And whatever you do, don't fall asleep. You will get very sunburnt. I know of two people who did. It was two girls at totally two different times. The first was a girl on her eighth grade field trip. The class went to a local lake for the day. The young girl got burnt on her back. It was so bad she had trouble wearing clothes. All she could wear was a halter top. However, when her back started to peel, her sisters had fun. They would have her lie on the floor so they could peel the skin off her back. The next girl was staying with her aunt for a while. She decided to lie out in the backyard. You guessed it—she went to sleep and got burnt. She got burnt worse than her mother did many years before.

Don't leave matches out where kids can find them, and believe me, age doesn't matter. A family living in a two-story apartment learned that lesson. There were three children. Two of them were downstairs playing, and the oldest of the children wanted to make a fire. She took some tissues and matches up to her bedroom. She lit a match and started the tissues on fire. Now the fire she made was in her nightstand drawer, beside her bed. It just so happened that the dad was on his way upstairs. He got a whiff of something; he wasn't sure what it was. So he went to her room; she was the only one upstairs. The smell was stronger in there. He asked her what she was doing, and she said nothing. There was a small bit of smoke coming out of the drawer, and so he opened the drawer carefully to find a pile of smoldering tissues. They didn't burn well. The fire didn't out of the drawer, so no harm was done to the room or the drawer. However, I do believe that a rear end did get warmed up and grounded after that.

If you ride your bike, don't ride double, unless you have a bike built for two. Here's why. A young man was riding one day, and a young lady asked him for a ride. Of course, he said yes. I'm calling him a young man because he was being a gentleman. As they were riding, they came to a steep hill. At the bottom of the hill, there was a short flat area, and beyond that was a busy street. The young man was standing on the pedals with the young lady sitting on the seat. They knew that they had to stop before they got to the road, so the front brakes were being used. No one is sure what happened. Did the brakes grab or the tire hit a rock or a pothole? The bike flipped the two off. The young man was sliding down the hill on his hands and stomach with the young lady sitting on him like he was a sled. He was the only one hurt. It took quite some time for his road rash to heal; that is what it is called when you get scrapped up on the road. Sometimes there can be little pieces of gravel or rocks that are in there; they have to be washed out or picked out. *Ouch!*

Curious young people need to be watched. Don't leave your straight pins where they can find them. I say this because I know of a child who found one and experimented with it. He was curious as to what would happen if a person was to stick a pin in an electrical cord. He took the pin to his room and sat on the floor by an outlet with his boom box. Of course, the box was plugged in. You can probably guess what he did. You are right, he stuck the pin in the cord while it was plugged in. His dad was in the garage working, and the lights went out. He went into the house to see if the lights in there were out also. He was headed downstairs to the fuse box to see if there was something wrong. At the bottom of the stairs was his son's bedroom. The boy was sitting there with a shocked look on his face. The boom box, however, didn't survive the experiment. No harm to the boy, except what his dad might have caused (not really harm but warming).

There is even a don't for adults. Did you know that if you took the works of a small gas grill and put them in a bigger grill, it doesn't work? I know someone who tried it. She had a hard time getting it to light. But finally, she got it lit, so she left it alone for a while. When she went back to check on it, something bad happened. She thought that the fire went out. As the grill was opened, somehow the gas ignited. Flames came out and burned her hand as she opened the lid and singed her eyebrows off. But that isn't all that got burnt. She smelled burning hair; it has a smell all its own. Her forehead was getting hot—her bangs were on fire. As she reached up to put them out with her burnt hand, it got burnt more. The worst part came later when her husband got home. He asked how it happened, and she told him. And for years he told the story to all their friends.

This starts out with a do: do help out a friend's wife when he is away with her car problems. She may bring it to your house and leave it so you can work on it. Here comes the don't: be very careful after you get it fixed and take it out for a test drive. Look behind you and make sure that nothing is in the way. Stop, let it soak in. Don't be backing up and realize too late that your car is in the way. You may run into it and damage the hood. Then you have to tell on yourself to your insurance agent so you can get your car fixed. And don't let them blame the owner of the friend's vehicle because it was all your fault.

Don't back up the car too fast. Let me explain. A woman was sent by her husband to get a part for the kitchen stove. The drawer wouldn't stay on track, so the wife, being a good wife, went to get the part. As she was leaving with the $9 part, she had to back out of her parking spot. As she was backing up, she said to herself, *Watch out for the big black pole.* And as she was thinking this, the big black pole jumped out and hit the back of the car. She went home and told her husband she had been attacked by the pole. He didn't believe the story. The couple had to pay the deductible on their insurance. The stove part after that cost $259. Some expensive part, don't you think? So when you back up, make sure you know where all the big black poles are so none can jump out and attack your car.

This is to all you cooks out there: if or when you make your spouse's favorite meal, be careful. I know a woman who made her husband's favorite meal for no special reason. There was fried chicken, mashed potatoes, gravy, and green beans. There was also a hot pumpkin pie in the oven. They ate their meal—mmmm, it was good! Desert time came, and the wife pulled the pie out and cut it. She served the first piece to her husband (she really didn't like pumpkin pie very much, so she didn't have a piece). Her husband took the first bite and said he had never tasted anything like this before. The wife was curious as to what made this pie different, so to her husband's surprise, she cut a piece for herself. He knew the pie tasted nasty, but he didn't want to make her feel bad. She took a bite and spat it out and said it was nasty. The best they could figure out was that she had forgotten to put the sugar in the pie. Another don't is, don't leave the room and forget about something cooking on the stove. It could be a disaster.

If you are having a war with the kids in the house, don't shoot your spouse. There was a man who was playing war with his sons in the house. They were shooting each other with toy guns that shot little yellow balls. Yes, they hurt some if you got hit. The mom had to cross the hall where they were playing. As she crossed the hall, she got shot. Believe it or not, her husband shot her on purpose. When she found out he aimed to do it, the chase was on. She chased him through the kitchen and into the living room. Then he got the idea to jump over the couch. He didn't make it; his top half made it, but one of his legs scraped across the back of the couch on its way over. And as to the time this was written, the scar can still be seen. So don't shoot your spouse and then attempt to jump over the couch. *Just don't shoot them!*

There was a hungry soldier who came home to an empty house. His wife and kids had already left for church. He was to meet them there after he ate. As he entered the house, all he could smell was chicken; he hoped his wife had left some chicken for him. All he saw was an empty plate on the floor; it must have been for the dog. Remember, I said he was hungry, so he looked in the fridge for some leftovers to eat. No luck. But there were some eggs, so he grabbed three and put them in a bowl in the microwave to cook. While they were cooking, he went to go change out of his uniform into regular clothes. While changing he heard three *pop, pop, pop* close together. He wondered what it could be. When he got to the kitchen, he found the source of the noise. The eggs in the microwave had exploded—what a mess. He didn't make it to church that night; he was busy cleaning. When his wife and kids got home, she asked he how the chicken was. His response was, what chicken? She told him about the three pieces she had left on a plate on the counter. You guessed it: the dog ate it. So don't leave food on the counter. Put it where the dog can't get it. Wonder if he knows how to open the microwave or fridge?

Don't let the kids and their mom pick out the family dog. The family wanted a dog. They looked in the paper and found someone giving away puppies. The ad said they were Boston terrier-cocker spaniel puppies. So it was agreed upon that the family would get one. The kids and their mom went and picked one out. That evening when dad got home, the kids excitedly showed off their new puppy. Dad said the dog looked just like a pit bull. After many years of having the pit bull in the family, they had to sadly get rid of him. Remember, don't let the kids and their mom pick out a dog. It happened again. The family wanted another dog. They wanted a small lapdog. The kids and mom went to a veterinarian that had puppies up for adoption. Now you would think that the vet would know one kind of a dog from another. Well, they adopted a cute little dog. The vet said it was a beagle. Well, in Tennessee language, that means big-o-dog. The family was living in Tennessee at the time. The dog grew. He weighed about sixty-five to seventy pounds when he grew up. He was not just a one lapdog; he was a two-lap dog.

Don't tell your two small sons that the urinals and toilets that flush themselves have a secret. The secret is that the sensors are holes that a little old lady peeks through. She is going to flush for you.

Don't try to keep a dog that doesn't want to be kept. Some dogs don't like to be a one-family dog. This one dog kept running away from his family. One time after being gone about a week, he came home with five or six different kinds of rope tied to his collar. He was then locked in the garage while the family went to church. He was in the driveway waiting for them when they got home. It seemed he ate a hole in the siding that was on the garage. So they tried a locked cage made of chain-link fence in a locked garage in a fenced yard with a locked gate. He got out by eating a hole in the cage and another hole in the siding on the garage. He again met them in the driveway. One other time after he run away, he was caught or turned into the Humane Society. They called to say he was there; the owner warned them that he would escape. They assured him his dog was safe and would be there in the morning. In the morning, a call came that somehow the dog had escaped in the night. This didn't happen just once but twice. The dog finally ran off and never came back.

Don't go hunting alone or with your young son, out in the woods. You may fall, or something may happen, and you may need to be carried out. Your young son might not be able to find his way out or be able to get his dad to the car. There wouldn't have been anybody there to drive to the hospital. Find a buddy or partner to go with you. Like we tell our kids, it is safer to be in twos. Who's your buddy?

Don't leave two chocolate cakes and a big bowl of homemade chocolate-covered pretzels on the kitchen table when the dog is left in the house and you are gone. You may find the empty bowl on the floor when you get home, and there may only be half of each cake left. It may not be a good idea to take the two halves of the cakes and make one for a family get-together.

Don't get so mad you rip a door off its hinges. One person thought someone was holding the door shut so she couldn't get in the house. She pushed and pushed on the door. Oops, the door opened the other way; somehow she ended up ripping the door off its hinges. No one was holding the door; her brothers would never do anything like that.

Kids, don't tell your teacher that your parents beat you when it was only a spanking that you deserved. The law says they are to turn it into the Department of Children's Service. That means they will check into the matter. You and your siblings could be taken away from your parents. That means you may never get to see them again.

Also, your parents could be put in jail if found guilty. It could also have some affect in their present employment and future employment even if found innocent.

If you're thinking about having all your grandchildren spend the night at the same time, check the weather first. I know a couple with thirteen grandchildren who didn't check the weather. It was going to be a stormy night with chances of tornadoes. The kids were all scared and crying, and the grandparents were afraid there would be a tornado. They didn't want anyone to get hurt. They all went down to a small dimly lit basement. The same couple also took all their kids and grandkids canoeing on a river. The grandpa told one of his daughters-in-law that the canoe wouldn't turn over. Guess what, it did turn over.

Oh, and, people, whatever you do, don't get hooked on the internet. It comes in many forms, believe me. To name a few—Facebook, games, tweeting, Snapchat, eBay, Amazon shopping, and all the other you-have-to-have-it-now places. There may be one bigger than that. Just about every family has one; some people even have them in the bedroom. That's a TV. That was, at one point in my life, the thing to have; almost everyone had at least one. Did you know a person can get hooked on soap operas, movies, cooking shows, DYI shows, house-flipping shows, and just about any other show a person can think of? Then there is being hooked on shopping. It could be just shopping by itself or shopping for a certain item. Oh, you can get hooked on good things too, like chocolate, food, chocolate, chips, chocolate, and I think maybe even writing this. Did I mention chocolate? Getting hooked on something just means you do it or eat it a lot, or it could be said a bunch—just don't overdo it on stuff. In the summertime, don't get hooked on air-conditioning. Yes, it is cool and feels good, but you should spend some time outside also. The early mornings or late evenings are the two times I find best: they are cooler.

Parents, don't put too much yeast in the homemade root beer. If you do, don't let the kids drink it; they may get drunk from it. Not good to get your four-year-old, or any age person, drunk.

LIFE STORIES | 53

And some of the biggest *don'ts* of all are—don't do drugs! *Don't* forget to tell your family and friends how much you love and appreciate them. *Don't* disobey to laws of the road! Or any laws. And Papaw says, *don't* forget Jesus loves you!

Driving Lessons

There are two people who got a lesson almost the same time in the same car. One was inside the car and one inside the house. Here is what happened: A mother and three children went to visit family. It was a sister-in-law and her two boys. After they arrived and parked the car on the driveway, they went in to visit. The kids wanted to go out and play; the weather was nice. Both moms agreed if the boys stayed in the yard. It was thought that the four were old enough to go unsupervised. Ha-ha, were they ever wrong.

The boys, all four of them, liked cars. The youngest boy of the visiting family decided to go for a drive—just pretend, he thought. When they had arrived, his mom parked the car in the driveway beside the house, not thinking she didn't put on the emergency brake. Her son climbed into the car, and as he did, he knocked the car out of park. Now this would have been no big deal, except the driveway was on a hill. As the moms glanced out the house window, they noticed the car was moving backward down the driveway. Both moms ran out of the house. Just as they got outside, the car went across the street and into the dirt bank of the house across the street. The car's name was Noisy. He was a brown 1969 Ford Mustang GT. What a pretty car he was. The only damage to the car was it got a tailpipe full of dirt. No one was hurt, just scared. So if you park on a hill, driveway or not, don't forget to put on the emergency brake. Well, just say if the vehicle can be knocked out of park or out of gear, put on the emergency brake to be on the safe side, no matter where you park.

Driving

There was a couple who traveled a lot. It was part of the dad's job. Well, anyway, his job took them all to Germany. The dad went over first. Then the family followed a few months later (that was the mom and their three children). The family got to take their car with them—well, I don't mean on the same plane. After they got settled in their apartment, they ventured out and found them a church they could go to. One day as they headed to church, they smelled something burning. The farther they went, the stronger the smell got. The dad said it was the car. The rear end was on fire. They all got out of the car very fast when they got to the church. There were flames coming out from under the back end of the car. It was on fire; dad was right. They hunted for something to put water in to put the fire out. All they could find was a bucket, the kind to make sandcastles with. It didn't work very well. Only the car got hurt. So they had to find a different car. A family that they knew were leaving, going back to the US. Now this family had a car they wanted to sell, so the other family bought it.

Now we can get to the driving part. The car was brown, and it was a Subaru. Somehow the car got the name Dusty. It had a manual transmission. That means it was a stick-shift car. Well, when the family left for the US, they took the car back with them (again it wasn't on the same plane). The family had the car a long time. I know this because the oldest child was taught how to drive it, and their second child learned three years later how to drive it. And three years after that, their third child learned to drive it. So with that said, that means all three teenagers learned to drive a stick shift in the same car, but not at the same time. Yes, he was a good, strong car to go through all that. He was also the family car. That means he was driven a lot in the years in between the children learning to drive him. I think there might have been some tears shed when they finally sold him. I know at least one of them who shed some. I know that may sound silly, but that is just the way some people are, and that is okay.

Empty Nests

After the kids have grown and moved away from home, that's called an empty nest. You might be surprised what some parents do. Some may travel, some may stay at home and vegetate, some may go shopping. Oh, to have control of the remote again; then they can watch anything on TV they want for as long as they want. They can listen to the music they like at the volume they like. They could even stay in their pajamas all day if they wanted to. They also can stay up as late as they want and get up anytime they want. As for shopping, there are flea markets, yard sales, estate sales, antique shops, and thrift shops. And I'm sure others know of other places to shop.

I know of one couple who took up hunting. They went deer, squirrel, and turkey hunting. They may hunt other things too, I don't know. They have a great friend who takes them to special hunting sites. He is a very good friend; he is more like a brother—in fact, he is a brother in Christ. Sometimes they didn't even care if they saw what they were hunting. That means they didn't get to shoot anything or even at anything. It can be enjoyable to have a conversation without someone interrupting. It can also be enjoyable to just sit and do nothing. Well, not really doing nothing. There's always God's creation to look at and enjoy.

There was another couple who went out and hunted for lamps. They had to go to flea markets and antique shops. Not electric lamps but oil lamps. There are some other names for these lamps also. They got the lamps to use when the power was out. They also wanted to give each of their children a lamp one day.

Everyone always talks about how lonely it will be after the kids are all moved out and gone—and how quiet it will be. Some don't find it that way at all. Yes, they love and miss their kids, but they are kinda glad that they are gone. They can do anything they want. They can go when they want to go, where they want to go, and stay as long as they want to. Or even just spend all day sitting around in their pajamas and do two things: diddly and squat. For some of you, that means to do nothing. And they can eat anything anytime they want and as much as they want. They can even have ice cream or chips anytime; it can even be the only thing they eat for a meal or all day.

 I myself am not sure what an empty nest is supposed to feel like, and that is because it is different for each and every couple. It can also be different for each person in a couple. And that is okay because we all are different from each other. God made us that way. So when it's your turn for the empty nest, enjoy yourself. Make some good memories. Have fun. Enjoy life!

Family Reunions

Some families have a reunion every year; others don't have any at all. All families are different. A family reunion should be a good time spent with all your family, or at least most of the family. Of course, you may not know all of them very well; you may only see them at family reunions. Some family reunions last a few hours, and some last a week. Some family reunions may be small, but some may have hundreds of family members present. Here's one example of a family reunion.

There was a small family reunion. It was a couple and their kids and grandkids. They wanted to spend several days together. Someone came up with the idea of a camping-trip reunion. It was all set up for a weekend in June. After they all arrived at the group campsite, the setting up started. A group campsite is an area with several campsites away from the others (more private that way). Tents went up, a camper was backed into a spot and leveled, and two pickup beds were turned into sleeping beds. Let me tell you about the two truck beds: One truck was backed up not far from a tree; there was a reason for that. A mattress was put in the bed to make a bed. A rope was tied to the center of the front bumper and taken over the cab and bed of the truck and tied to a tree. Then a tarp was hung over the rope. This made sort of a tent over the bed. Not a bad idea. There was even a small light hung on the rope. Now the other truck was set up in a totally different way. It was just parked at a campsite. The truck had a top on its bed. Some call it a topper, some a camper shell. It wasn't quite tall enough to stand up in.

An air mattress was spread out and inflated, and sleeping bags and covers were spread out on top of it. Jackets and long pants were laid out and ready to put on. The man from the first truck went over to see how things were going at the other truck. You see, he was the dad and papaw of the family. He asked his son-in-law about all the blankets. He then reminded him it was the middle of June. The answer wasn't quite what he expected. It was explained to him that there was a family curse on him. It seems that every time someone from his family goes camping, strange things happen. They both went on and didn't think about it anymore. In the morning when everyone got up, some of them were cold. Some were sitting around a fire trying to get warm; others were sitting wrapped up in blankets. The curse showed itself again. The state hit the record low that night for that time of the year.

It seems no one learned from that experience. Several years later, another family reunion camping trip was planned by the same families. Everyone got there and set up, had supper, and then went to sleep that night. When they all got up warm in the morning, they talked about what they all were going to do that day. The sun was shining, and a breeze was blowing. The weather seemed perfect for camping, not too hot and definitely not too cold. They were beginning to think that there wasn't a curse. After breakfast, the sky turned dark, and the wind began to blow hard. The rain came pouring down. Everyone gathered up under a tarp hanging from the trees to make shade for the picnic tables. The curse showed itself again.

And after experiencing the curse twice, the kids, now adults, still had at least one more camping family reunion after the grandparents both had passed away. Oh, and on that camping reunion trip, it rained and rained; flash-flood warnings were put out for the area. One of their tents leaked; the camper top leaked. Remember the truck with the camper top? The bed was a bed, and over half of them got wet during the night. Some of the nearby roads were underwater; some campsites were also underwater. Someone said they saw an ark float by. The curse struck again.

Fire Trucks

This is two stories in one. The first starts with a man and his wife going to a cruise-in. They went there to look at the old cars. There was a man there selling raffle tickets to help a local volunteer fire department. The man and his wife just wanted to donate some money to the cause. The volunteer fireman would not take it; he said they had to purchase the raffle tickets. The man got the raffle tickets. He didn't give them a second thought. Several weeks later, he got a call from the man at the fire department. He had won. He asked what he had won. The answer was a firetruck or a hundred dollars. Everyone in the past had always chosen the money, so it was not a new truck, but it was still in the box and never driven. The man picked the truck. The truck was a pedal truck. It had "Volunteer Fire Department" printed on the side. The man thought it would be great for his granddaughter to drive around in. Of course, she would have to grow some first.

His granddaughter enjoyed the truck for years till she outgrew it. It was then put back in its box for many years till another granddaughter came along. Now she has outgrown the truck also. So back in the box. I guess it may be waiting for a great-grandchild to come along.

Now the other firetruck story. A man went to a flower shop and got his mother some flowers: a nice arrangement in the back of a little metal firetruck. As the health of his mother passed, she started giving things to her kids that she had gotten from them in the past. She asked if he wanted the truck. He took it, and now almost every week his granddaughter plays with it. She has little dolls that drive the firetruck all over the coffee table. The truck has its own parking spot in the living room.

Flies and Lightning

A family moved to Alaska. There were three children. The children's ages were six and three years old. The youngest child was only six weeks old. Fast-forward. The family moved back to the lower forty-eight states three years later. The trip was a long one, about seven days long. One day they stopped in Montana to get something to eat. While sitting in a restaurant, a fly landed on the now three-year-old's arm. He started crying and screaming like someone was killing him. The waitress rushed over to see what was wrong. It was explained to her that a fly had landed on him. He had never seen a fly before; he didn't know what it was or what it was going to do.

Further down the road when the family stopped so they could visit with relatives, there was a thunder and lightning storm. The three-year-old just stood on the porch and watched, amazed. The grandpa asked if something was wrong. It was explained to him that was the boy's first time to hear thunder and see lightning. No flies, thunder, or lightning in Alaska to see or hear—that's right. Remember the boy was only six weeks old when they moved up there. That was the only place he remembered living in. If it had been a mosquito that landed on him or the Northern Lights, he would have been okay; he knew what they were.

God Loves Us

We all should know 1 John 4:10: "God loved us and sent His Son." What a simple thought. We all should have heard this or something like it, but have we really? Did we just hear it, or did we just listen to it? There is a big difference. Who are we? Why does God love us? Who is His Son, and where did He get sent to and why? We are all sinners and not very nice people at times. Of course, some are worse than others. But are they really? Do any of us deserve to be loved? Think about it! A sin is a sin. So telling a little white lie is just as bad as killing someone. Right? So why would God send His Son? Can He love a world full of bad people that much? Oh, you say, He didn't know we were going to be that bad when the world was created. But believe it or not, He did. And He sent Jesus to earth for us anyway—to be tortured, beat, and hung on a cross for us. He could have done it differently. It really took a lot of love from both of Them to do all this. I say *both* because Jesus knew all this was going to happen to Him. But He still came to the earth for us. Yes, He left heaven and His Father for all of us. And so what do we do to show our love for Him? Or do we even love Him? Or do we even care about it? Or do we even believe it?

God's Gifts

These are the gifts that God gives to us. Let's start with the first one: the gift of life. Some may say their parents gave them life. Others say that it is a gift from God. Your mom did give birth to you, but God gives you life. God also gave His Son, Jesus, to us. That means He also gives everyone the chance to have eternal life. All you have to do is accept it. The how is—know Jesus as your Lord and Savior. Now let's get back to the gift of life. Have you ever wondered how it's possible for a baby to develop and grow inside a woman? All things are possible with and through God. After your birth, you continue to grow, physically and mentally. I guess that all just happens. I don't think so.

What about speech? Some are good at speaking in front of crowds, and others are not. That's the gift of speech. God gives most everyone some kind of gift of speech. I say most because some people are born without the ability to speak. But they can speak in other ways, like sign language. That is a gift from God. Can you hear? Some can't hear. That is also a gift from God. Hearing or not, both are gifts. If you can hear, make sure you listen. There is a difference. But if you can't hear, there are other ways to know what others say. There's sign language—yes, it's good, for both the ones who can't speak and the ones who can't hear. Isn't it amazing how that works out? It is a gift from God.

The ability to talk to others easily is also a gift from God. You ask how? Okay, let us say you grow up and become a preacher. You should be able to talk with anyone easily. But not just talk, you also have to make sense. Some people just go on and on and don't say anything. That isn't a gift from God.

There are so many, many more gifts that God gives us. Here are just a few more: teaching, praying, listening, being a shoulder to cry on, discernment, service, preaching, being a good parent and good grandparents, being a source of encouragement to someone. And there are many, many more. So find what your gift or gifts are and *use* them. Yes, I said *gifts*. God may bless you with more than one gift. So if you find one, keep looking. There may be more to find. And guess what, as you grow in the Lord, or older, your gifts may multiply or change. That means there may be more, so keep looking even if you don't think you can do more. God is there to help you at all times with all things. All you have to do is pray, listen, and take the path of life He wants you to follow. It is that easy to do, if you let Him guide you. Don't try the path you think is right. Pray and know if it is the right one. I forget to tell you the last and final gift: the gift of being in heaven with Him forever and ever.

Growing Up

My parents were different from most parents. They didn't show their love for each other very much. We always teased them about the Christmas kiss. That was the only time of the year that we saw them kiss. As kids at bedtime, it was a little bit like *The Waltons*. That was a TV show about the Walton family. We didn't say everybody's name, but we did say, "God bless you, night-night."

There's a story about my older sister and myself when we were young. We were both riding on one tricycle. I was standing on the back. We were just riding around and around on the front porch one evening. As kids that didn't last long, so we were sitting or maybe lying down on the porch. Mom opened the door and said, "Get up off that cold porch!" We instantly got up, and both got back on the tricycle. This time, when we wanted to trade places, the driver would back up to the doorway. The one on the back would stand in the doorway. Then the other one would also stand in the doorway; then we would get back on. We didn't get on the cold porch again that night. And believe it or not, we still got in trouble. Mom said we knew what she meant about staying off the cold porch.

We would also get in trouble for driving her clothespins into the ground. We were just trying to make a tent. We would throw a blanket over the swing set or clothesline and stake it to the ground. It worked when we got away with it. Not very often did that happen.

The year mom got a washing machine in the box, we got in trouble again. We made a playhouse, hiding place, cave, and many other places out of it. You can do a lot with a box and an imagination. Dad said we liked and played with the box more than playing with any of our new toys.

It seems that we always had cats, or at least there were some around. One time we had a cat that was in the family way. That wasn't right; she wasn't married. We hunted down a male cat for her to marry, and we performed a wedding for her. We did this standing beside our house. Most of the time, all the cats had names. As I said, it seemed we always had cats. One time I remember that we had three momma cats that all had kittens at the same time or about the same time. And they all were under the rose bush together. The kittens didn't mind which momma fed them. That made the total number of cats around seventeen, too many to name. I remember several of the cats being mine. There was Diane. She was a black cat, and she got run over. There was Two Eyes. He was a white cat with one blue eye and one green eye. And I know there may have been others I don't remember.

We lived out in the country on a gravel road, and sometimes we would go riding our bikes up and down the road. One of my little sisters would crash and skin up her knees almost every time she went riding. She never got the hang of turning in or out of the gravel driveway.

One year, my older sister and myself got to paint the garage door. My older sister and I also painted each other. A little green paint here and a little white paint there. Was kind of hard getting it out of clothes and hair and off our faces. We got in trouble for that too. I don't understand; we did a good job.

I would also make up stories at bedtime to help one of my little sisters get to sleep. Oh, I did make up stories for other things also. I got in trouble for that. The bedtime stories were kinda silly at times. I guess they were boring stories because she did go to sleep during the story, not after it was over.

There were several times I got into trouble. I did that a lot, as you can see. Some people say that I have grown up physically but not mentally. To some extent, that may be true about all of us. Don't you have a little kid in you wanting to get out sometimes? Some people have more little kid in them than others. But I think that is what keeps life interesting. So remember, parents, what all you did growing up the next time your kids do something that gets them in trouble. I still get in trouble sometimes.

Gummies

There once was a family that lived in Germany. Okay, there was more than one family living there. But this story is about one family. The parents and their three kids. The family was moved over there by the dad's work. They lived in an apartment building. The basement served storage rooms. Each apartment had a room. On the first and second floors, there were twelve apartments, six on each floor. The third floor was just three big rooms that could be used for meetings, parties, or a place for the kids to play on a rainy day.

Now to get to the gummies part. At each end of the building was a dumpster. One day the three kids were outside playing. They spotted a lady digging in one of the dumpsters. She seemed to be finding a lot to put in a bag she had. Being, curious the kids went over to see why she was going through the trash. She told them that she had family on the other side of the wall. The kids knew that there was a wall called the Berlin Wall, and it divided Germany in two. The lady told them her name was Mrs. Muller. She was going through the trash to find stuff to send to her family. "Americans are so wasteful," she told them. Her family would be happy to get the clothes, toys, and other stuff that was still halfway good. She told the kids that if they wanted to, they could help her get the stuff to her house. The kids asked their mom if they could; she said yes. You could trust most people at that time. Mom was glad the kids wanted to help.

When they got to Mrs. Muller's house, she gave them a quarter for helping her. She then told them the way to the gummy store. There were all kinds of candy there, mostly gummies. That quarter got them a small bag of candy. All sizes of kids love candy, all kinds of candy. From then on, the kids would collect things to take to her so they could buy themselves some more gummies, if she gave them money again. Mrs. Muller was a very nice person. She invited the whole family over for tea one day. The mom and kids went and had a nice time. Dad was at work, so he couldn't go. After the family moved back to the U S, the kids still talked about the candy and Mrs. Muller. I believe they still do. I know that they still do. In 2019, the subject of a modern gummies commercial came up, and one of the kids, now grown with a family of his own, said something about the gummy store. A new conversation was started with his sister about the gummy store and its candy.

Hamburgers

There was a family that moved back to the parents' home town. They did this so the mom and kids would be close to family. The dad wouldn't be there; he had to go work somewhere else. His job was sending him away for a year. The family thought it would be a good thing to buy a home for the mom and three kids to live in while the dad was gone. The plan was that after the dad retired, they could move back and live there. That would be quite a few years later. After they got all settled in, they knew dad would have to leave sometime. The time came, and dad was gone. But only for a year. His job sent him away a lot.

The family went to McDonald's on a Wednesday for lunch. The place was very busy that day; most of the time, it wasn't that busy. They found out why: on Wednesday, hamburgers were only $0.10, and cheeseburgers were $0.15. What a deal. Only one catch: there was a limit of ten per customer. The mom had a way around that. Each Wednesday, they all would go to McDonald's, and each one would get ten hamburgers. They didn't eat all forty of them at once. They would freeze some of them and pull them out for after-school snacks or just a little snack anytime. When the burgers were microwaved for thirty seconds, they would come out just like a fresh one.

There was one day the kids' cousin came over after school. Of course, the boys were hungry. So they got them some burgers out and warmed them up. Their cousin wanted a second one, so he got it and put it in the microwave for forty-five seconds. Now remember that wasn't the right time. Well, when he took the hamburger out, it was extrahot, and he hollered, "Ouch!" So after that, forty-five seconds was called the ouch time. Not just for hamburgers but for everything.

Hunting

Some people love to hunt. To some, hunting is going to the woods and sitting there. You go and sit in the woods for hours and hours at a time. Don't get me wrong, it can be enjoyable—sitting in the woods just waiting for something to come along so you can shoot it. You can listen to the birds singing and see them flying all around. You could also hear and maybe see a hawk or two. You also can hear the woodpeckers pecking and maybe get to see one or two of them. Then there is watching the chipmunks and squirrels hunting food or digging in the ground and making all kinds of sounds. If you are lucky, you could see a red fox or some other animals. There also may be butterflies go flitting by every now and then. You could write stories or read books or work in a puzzle book or play games on your phone. But just sitting there and listening to all of nature is very, very relaxing. You can also catch up on some sleep. That means it's so peaceful you might fall asleep. I know a couple who does that a lot. They take turns napping so they don't miss seeing anything.

Oh, this is supposed to be about hunting, that's right. Well, while you are sitting there waiting and watching for the right animal to come along so you can shoot it, you may kinda be bored. That is hunting. That's where all the other stuff above comes in. Don't get me wrong, it may be enjoyable, but it would be better if you got to shoot something while hunting. That is why it's called hunting, not shooting. Also, it helps if the right animal shows up. You may see deer while hunting turkeys, or turkeys while hunting deer. That means you are not supposed to shoot them; it's not the right season. The animals that you're hunting may also show up but stay far enough away that you can't shoot them. That's frustrating! Hunting can also be dressing in layers and layers of clothes and then still freezing anyway. You could also dress in layers and layers of clothes and not need them; the weather could get too warm for all those clothes. You are never sure what to wear or how much to wear.

I Felt Alone

At a time of loss in my life, I felt alone. I felt no one knew what I was going through or how I felt. I felt no one—I mean no one—had ever felt this way. I was the only one that felt this way, and no one really cared. I felt no one else even noticed. If I had known about all the people who were praying or even just thinking of me, I wouldn't have felt that way. I would have felt crowded in a gigantic space. But there was someone there with me that I couldn't see, but He knew what I was going through. He cared. He noticed me. Yes, it was God. I was reminded of this by a song, "Leaning on the Everlasting Arms." So I know that even in the darkest of times, and the not-so-dark times, none of us are alone. We all have the arms of God right there just waiting to catch us and hold us and comfort us, if we let Him. What could be better than that. No matter how you feel, remember that you are never really alone. There is one who cares. It's okay to talk with Him. He will always listen. He is always there. He does care about all. It doesn't matter how good or bad you have been; He is always there for you.

Left Behind

Did you know that there was a series of movies made with that name? This isn't about those movies. This is about a couple and their kids. They were involved in a church and its youth group. One morning they drove the youth to an event in the church bus. Okay, only the dad drove. The couple had three children (that is an important part of the story). Late that night when they got back to the church, they all were tired. However, some of the youth needed a ride home, and some were picked up by parents. So the ones who needed a ride all piled into the church van. And off the family went to take the kids home.

It took quite some time to get them all home. When the family got back to the church, the oldest child asked where the middle child was. Why she only noticed then that he was missing, no one knows. They looked all over the van and didn't find him. Okay, just the inside of the van. That didn't take long. They started to worry that they had left him at the event miles and miles away. But then they remembered that he did get on the bus after the event. So they searched the bus, and there he was, curled up on one of the back seats. He had been there asleep the whole time they were delivering the other kids home, probably a couple hours or so. The best they can figure out is that he slept there all that time by himself on the bus, alone in the dark. He didn't even know that he had been left behind, forgotten by his family. You didn't hear anything about the youngest child because he was asleep in his mom's arms the whole time. Well, maybe not in her arms but leaning on her. They don't believe that the child was affected by this mentally because he didn't know about it when it happened.

Jesus Gifts

This isn't what some may call a gift. It is a special gift. Let me explain. You see, this married couple always had trouble coming up with what they wanted for Christmas. So they got the idea to give Jesus a gift since Christmas is about Him, right? They each prayed to God for what He wanted their gift to be. When they knew what it would be and where it would go, it was the spouse's responsibility to make it happen. Over the years, the gifts came in many forms. I will tell you about two. The first one was the husband's gift. He wanted to give each person on the Coast Guard cutter *Harriet Lane* a Christmas gift. He was given that idea because their son was assigned to that ship. The ship was going out to sea and would be gone for Christmas and New Year's. His gift was to be cookies and other goodies for them.

However, he didn't know that it was one hundred and ten people on the ship when he was given the idea. So his wife took on the task. She would pick up some boxes every time she had to go to the post office. It took quite a few trips to get that many boxes. Her husband, daughter, and granddaughter helped her make and cut out sugar cookies. They made a dozen for each person. That wasn't the only kind of cookies that they made; there were two other kinds. There were all kinds of goodies for them also. There was candy, noisemakers, elf ears to wear, cups with reindeers or snowmen on them, and lots of other goodies. Now the question was how to get all the items in the boxes.

They made sort of an assembly line. The boxes were lined up all around the living room. They were lined up on the couch, chairs, coffee table, and almost any other flat surface they could find except the floor (they had to be able to walk around). Now to get to filling them. Each person took a section of boxes to fill; then all the items were passed around one at a time. And when that was done, each box was taped shut and wrapped in brown paper bags (thank you, Kroger). And instead of trying to mail all the boxes, the couple loaded up their car (it was really loaded up).

Off they went to take them to Virginia. Virginia was where the ship was docked when it wasn't out at sea. There is another gift I remember. The wife's gift was to take and give a truckload of clothes to the mountains. That was to a place in the mountains where they would be passed out to people that needed them. The mountains were in the far east part of their state. There were coal mines there that were shut down, so the people didn't have much.

The couple went to visit some family members one weekend. The wife and someone else went out to yard sales and found a good bargain. This one place was trying to get rid of all the clothes; they were a dollar a bag. Well, they started filling bags. They ran out of plastic grocery bags and started using garbage bags. The price was the same, no matter what size the bag was, and they really stuffed the bags full. Then they started loading up their pickup. They filled the whole back end of the truck for not much money. And then when the time came, they took the clothes to the mountains.

There are many more things that they have given Jesus for His birthday; this is just two. What do you give Him? Do you even think about Him on His birthday or any other time?

Life in the Army

There was this young couple and their kids. The word *kids* means "children." Dad loved his family and wanted to provide for them. But they lived in a small town, and dad couldn't find a job. So to provide for his family, he joined the army. As some of you know, the life of an army family is not always easy. There is a lot of moving from home to home. It is more than just house to house or place to place. It can be from state to state or country to country. Well, this family did move a lot. They moved fourteen times in the first fourteen years of being in the army. That was hard for the kids to make friends and then to have to leave them. But I think the hardest part was to go without a daddy around. Let me explain. The army required dad to be gone from his family a lot. Sometimes it was to go to a school in a different state or to the field, or wherever they wanted him to go. None of the family liked that part of the army life. They figured it up dad was away from his family fourteen out of the twenty years, he was in the army. They liked being able to see a lot of different things. Different countries and all the different places in the States.

Like I said, dad loved his family. So when he was home, he would do things with them. One time he took them sledding. Now this is different than most sledding. There wasn't any snow or sleds. It was on cardboard, and they slid down a hill covered with pine needles. Dad would also take time to play and do different things with them. They also went for picnics up on mountainsides. They did the usual things to like fishing, hunting, and sightseeing also. They went to parks with playgrounds to play and picnic. They even went on vacations. Most of the time, it was during spring break or fall break. I think daddy did a great job providing for the family. He supplied them with a home, food, and all that goes with it. But most important, he gave them his love and time. Even after getting out of the army, he still did things with his family. That is what daddies are supposed to do.

Life Isn't as Bad as You Think

You might not think you have a good life. Your house is small and crowded; you only have three bedrooms and a bath and a half. This is just for two people. It seems that there is cleaning or straightening to be done every day. The double garage is full and has no room for the cars. The lawn is so big it takes your whole Saturday to get it cut and trimmed—and all the time it takes to keep it looking nice the rest of the year. If you didn't have all that to do, how much extra time would you have. There is only so many hours in a day. It is your choice on how you spend them.

Oh, the alarm clock goes off. You don't want to get up. What a day ahead. Work, work, and more work. Well, at least you woke up; you are not dead. Where are you? In your own house, in your own bed, in the hospital, in ICU, in jail? How is the temperature? Is the heat or air working? And as for work, at least you have a job. You are not depending on the charity of others. You have the ability to work. You are mentally and physically able to get up, dress yourself, feed yourself, and take care of yourself. And if not, you have someone willing to help you. You don't have it as bad as you think.

Ah, breakfast time. Do you choose to have toast, eggs, cereal, oats, or go out for a fast-food breakfast? Look at it this way, you can't have life too bad if you have these choices: you are not going out and picking something up out of the trash somewhere or to a soup kitchen or a street corner to beg for your breakfast. And don't forget about the food for the rest of the day. You probably do eat more than once a day, don't you?

Getting dressed for the day. What to wear? You go to the closet, and it is full of choices. The dresser and chest of drawers are full also.

You can't find anything to wear. Or is it you can't find anything you want to wear? You do at least have more than one set of clothes to wear, and they probably are in good shape and clean. How did they get clean? Do you have a washer and dryer? Does someone else come in and do the laundry for you? Where does the water, soap, and electricity come from? It could be as easy as putting the clothes in the washer with some soap, and then taking them out and putting them in the dryer. You don't have to go and look for handouts or go through the dumpsters somewhere.

Work! Yes, this can even be a blessing. You have a way to provide for yourself and your family, if you have one. It doesn't have to be a job that pays thousands of dollars a week. If you are wise with how you spend it, it will be enough. You don't have to have name brands or clothes with other people's names on them. If that is what you want, go to a secondhand store; sometimes some of the clothes will have a name on them. If you do have work to go to, that is better than having a corner to stand on, not knowing what or if anything will be given to you. It also should make you feel better to be able to show the rewards of your job. The reward is the paycheck you receive.

Not the newest, fastest, fanciest car sitting in the driveway. That is okay. At least there is a car for you to use. It is not that important how it looks as long as it gets you from one place to another. Just be thankful there is a car and that you don't have to walk or have to wait for a bus everywhere you want to go.

If you don't feel well, you should be thankful there are hospitals or doctors to go to. Yes, it can be time-consuming and expensive. But just think about it. If there were no hospitals or doctors, what would you do? There probably would be no medications to take either. You would just have to suffer through it all. No cures for the simplest things. Do your feet hurt? At least you have feet. Shoes too tight? At least you have shoes. Hands ache? At least you have hands. Oh, your aching back. At least you are able to feel pain.

Think you don't have a good life? Look around and see the others that really have a hard life. Be thankful for what you have. Is there anything you can do to help others? If you are serious about helping, you will find a way. If you can't find a way, ask others what you can do. Remember that person on the corner *is* a person. God made us all and loves all of us. Do your part to share His love with others. The least you could do no matter who you are is to wave or nod at that person and smile. A smile goes along way.

Life

It's so pleasant to wake up in the morning in my own bed, in my own house, with my own family nearby. I know there's food for breakfast. I have clothes and shoes to slip on, and I have a lot of stores and public services that I can go to and use. I can choose to pray or not to pray. I can choose to read my Bible or not to read it. I can choose to worship God or not to worship God.

What would it be like to be one of the many who wake up knowing there is no food for breakfast, or maybe the whole day? Or to wake up in a nasty cellar or prison or a mud hut? What would it be like to wake up cold and miserable, or to wake up in a hospital bed where waves of pain come over your body? What would it be like to have the choice—if you pray, you die? What about not being able to even own a Bible? What about not being able to openly worship God? I don't like or want to think about all of that, but I must.

As a Christian and as a member of humans, compassion must enter our hearts and minds and cause us to pray and then do something. You say I am just one person; what can I do to make any kind of difference? You can start with something as simple as praying every time you hear a siren. Pray for the driver of the vehicle to be kept safe. Pray for the situation they are headed to. Or you might pray for the driver of the car ahead or beside you and/or the car behind you. It doesn't have to be a long, complicated prayer, just something, and God will know what you're trying to say. Just pray. For some of you, that means talk *with* God, not just at Him.

What if you see someone on the street corner begging for food or money? How are you to know if they are really in need? Here is a way to find out: pray to God for guidance in what He would have you do. Easier than that, pray in the morning for guidance on what you are to do with the day God has given you.

Those are just a few simple ways to help your fellow human beings. There are more ways to be a better Christian and human being, but start where God wants you. The only way to find out is to pray and then listen for His answer. And then do it or go there!

Missing

One day a grandmother was waiting for her granddaughter to get off the school bus. This was at the bus stop by the girl's house. The grandmother got there early and was waiting. The bus came unloaded and started to leave, but her granddaughter wasn't there. The grandmother called mom to find out why she wasn't told there would be no granddaughter on the bus. Mom was very upset; her daughter should have been on the bus. The school was called and asked where the girl was. They didn't know. They contacted the bus; the driver said the girl had gotten off the bus at her house. But she didn't! So where was she? Mom was worrying where her daughter was. She went to the school to look for her daughter. Somehow the girl was mixed up with someone else and told she was to stay and take part in an after-school program. Mom found her and let the school know that the bus driver needed to keep better track of who was on the bus and who wasn't.

Several weeks later, the grandmother was the one missing. She had lain down to rest. To make sure she was up in time to get her granddaughter, she set an alarm. The time for the bus came and went. The granddaughter wasn't picked up. The girl called her mother. The mom called the grandmother many times, but no answer. The mom left work and went to pick up her daughter. They both wondered where the grandmother was. The mother feared something was wrong with the grandmother. As the mother and her daughter went into the grandmother's house, they found her there lying on the couch. She had the phone by her head and had slept through the alarm and all the calls. Oops!

LIFE STORIES | 85

My Family

I love my husband and all my kids and all my grandkids and great-grandkids—those I have met and those I haven't met.

My husband and I met when we were in high school. He is the only one I ever dated, and I am the only one he ever dated. My parents wanted me to go out with someone else so I would have someone to compare him with. He came up with the idea to have his best friend pick me up for a date. This was a trick. The friend would just take me to a spot and drop me off, where my future husband would be waiting. Then at an arranged time, we all would meet back together, and I would change cars; then the friend would take me home. My parents would think I went out with someone else. I did not like the idea. I did not want to trick my parents like that, so I never dated anyone else. No one else even asked or was interested in me, as far as I know.

My husband and I have had many years together. There had been rough spots, but we always made it through. Everyone asks what the secret to staying married so long is; the answer is *work*. Not get up and go to work for a paycheck. But if you did something for your spouse before you were married, keep doing it. Also, there all kinds of other things that can be done for each other. My husband opens doors for me—car, house, store, church, anywhere we go. He brings me flowers every week. Sometimes I will have more than one week of flowers on the table; some die quicker than others. But that doesn't matter. He will notice when my neck or back are bothering me and volunteer to rub them for me. He also does feet. In return, I do the same for him. Don't put yourself first; put others.

I love all our children. We would have had four but lost one to miscarriage. There is our daughter and two sons. The child we lost was between the boys. We also have an adopted daughter and currently six adults that have asked us to be their parents. Most of our kids live close. The two boys don't, but we try to see them when we get the chance. The adopted daughter has not been seen in years, her own doing. Ah, grandkids. There are nine grandchildren, only eight living. One grandchild has gone to be with the Lord.

One of our sons told me the other day that his daughter was like me. I asked him to explain. He told me that with her birthday money, she spent it making others happy. I enjoy doing and buying things for others too. Last but not least, there is one great-grandchild. I'm hoping for at least one more grandchild, but I expect there to be a lot of great-grandkids and great-great-grandkids in the future. We also have grown adults that have adopted us as parents, so our family continues to grow. I love the family God has given me. My favorite verse in the Bible is Philippians 4:4: "Rejoice in the Lord always and again I say rejoice." Be happy with your family and life no matter what happens.

My Parents

Hey, Mom, can you please take me out to Clyde Strow's place? I need to get my starter rebuilt. Mom, can I get a ride to Schaefer and Paulin's? I need a new battery? Hey, Dad, can I borrow the car? If only everyone had parents like I got. What a wonderful world this would be. All the wonderful times I had in my life because my parents cared for me so well, always putting us kids as number one in their lives. All the wonderful memories I have now because of that. I remember when I went for a walk one time, and Ray Arnold brought me back home. He was a policeman in our town. Mom grabbed me and hugged on me; it was as if I had run off or something! There was this time that I found out my dad was the greatest man alive. An old drunk threatened to throw gas on me and burn me up. My dad came after him, and I never had a problem with that guy again. Ya know, it's just like the time those two guys at Sewell's did catch me on fire. My dad took care of that too! He was great about that—he is the most courageous man I know, yet he also has a soft side to him.

One time, we were all in the car waiting on Mom to come out of P.N. Hirsh on Main Street, and all of a sudden Dad said, "Hey, kids, look at this really good-looking woman coming!" We all looked, and there was Mom. Cool, huh? He hugs us and tells us he loves us all the time—just don't get better than that. He always gave us kids 100 percent, and we had great lives for it. Couldn't always go places, but we still had fun. There were picnics in the backyard. The time, he would hose us down in the summer; it was great. And when we went anywhere, it was a great trip because Dad always took the most interesting routes. Then there was the wee-has! Those awesome hills! What a great time we always had.

I just wish I would have not been a goof when I grew up and caused so many problems for them two. Even when I messed up bad, like wrecking the car, the concern was for me, not the car. Dad even commented that he wrecked a car just down the hill from there. We knew we were going to the lake for the day when we got up and smelled fried chicken. Mom made a big picnic lunch and cookies for snacks. Mom made the best children and cookies. One time I came home, and she was crying while doing the dishes. I ask her why she was crying, and she told me because to have dirty dishes, there had to be food to put on them. When my kids say to me, "Thanks for raising me this way, Dad," I will tell them I had two of the greatest teachers for being a parent that anyone could have. Dad also had a kid's side to him, like the time we came back from fishin', and he turned an eel loose in Mom's bathwater. We did some snowball fights and sword fights in the dark with Dad. We took cardboard and made shields and swords and went to battle—oh, what fun it was. We went fishin', huntin', and swimmin' and just ridin' around in the country. Dad taught us how to fix things and make things and use our hands. My parents encouraged us in every way on how to succeed and to be content with whatever we had. Both of my parents were the best.

Mystery Illness

There was a woman and her husband who liked going to flea markets on Saturday. One Saturday, they got ready to go. After going to the flea market, they were going to visit some friends. The woman said she didn't feel well and asked if they could just go home. The next day at church, the woman said she didn't feel well and asked if they could go home. This was a very unusual request coming from the lady; her husband knew she must have really felt bad.

That Monday morning when the woman got up, her arms from the elbows to fingertips and her legs from the knees to the toes were swollen and almost black in color. This was not right. Off to the doctors they went. At the doctor's office, they didn't say what it was. They just took six tubes of blood and said go home, keep your hands and feet above your heart, and come back in a week. So for a week, all the lady did was lie on the couch with her hands and feet above her heart.

Having a husband and three teenagers in the house, there was a lot of things that went undone that week. The next week's doctors visit went about the same. The results of the blood work came back: there was nothing wrong. The lady was healthy. So she was told to give more blood and sent home and to keep her hands and feet above her heart again and come back in a week.

The husband went to his boss and asked for time off so he could take care of his wife and family, the boss was very understanding. He said to just go take care of things and to check in every few days with him. This went on for months. The doctors took two lymph nodes out of the lady's leg to run tests on them; they found no reason for her to be sick.

One Wednesday night, the kids went to church; the parents stayed home. The mom was upstairs in bed, and the dad was downstairs. He got the feeling something was wrong. As he went up the stairs, he could hear the mother breathing. It sounded like a dog panting after it had just run five miles. As he was getting her in the car, the kids arrived home. Off they went to the emergency room. At the hospital, they took her right in and hooked up to all kinds of monitoring machines. Her blood pressure was so high it was unreadable; her heart rate was sky high. The doctors called the dad in to spend time with her in her last minutes. Her heart was going to wear itself out. There, alone together, with all her strength, the mom told the dad that whatever happened, remember that she loved him, and so did God.

The beeping of the machines slowed down; this meant her heart was slowing down. Was this the end? The doctors came to check? The panting stopped, the blood pressure was coming down, the heart rate leveled off. She was doing fine. She was then sent to a nearby hospital by ambulance for a lung scan. When she arrived back in the emergency room, they hooked her back to the monitoring machines. At 6:00 a.m., they admitted her to the hospital. It was just so they could monitor her.

When the doctors did their rounds at 9:00 a.m., they said she was not sick enough to be in the hospital and sent her home. She was told again to keep her hands and feet above her heart. She would get depressed and have herself a little pity party; this was usually on a Saturday. Her husband would get her out to the car and take her for a ride. Most of the time, it was out in the country to see the wildlife and soak in to beauty of nature. This seemed to help. The dad also had put a lawn chair and a handheld shower head in the tub. You see, his wife could not stand for a very long at a time. She could not walk up or down the stairs; she had to crawl.

On one of the weekly doctor visits, it was said they wanted to send the lady to another hospital to see a specialist. This took place at another hospital. The doctor and her interns examined the woman and could not figure out what she had. At the end of the appointment, the doctor said that if they ever figure out what she had to please let her know. There was even a panel of doctors visiting the hospital that asked to see the lady. They were also puzzled by the illness.

One day the piano player from the church came over. She told the man to go do what he wanted that she would sit with his wife and take care of her if she needed anything. The dad got ready and went to work to check in and catch up on some paperwork. While at work, he kept thinking of his wife. He was emotionally drained from all of this. He shut the door to his office and got down on his knees and prayed. He prayed for healing, whether it be her getting well or God taking her home. When he finished, he got up wiped his face and opened the door.

As he was sitting at his desk, the phone rang. It was the piano player telling him he needed to come home now. On the drive home, he got to wondering what he would find. He imagined the worst: a coroner's car or ambulance parked in the driveway. As he arrived home, there was nothing like that in the driveway. As he walked into the house, all he heard was "Oh my!" over and over. As he walked into the living room, the two ladies were watching the swelling and color go away.

The next week's doctor's visit was different. Instead of going in a wheelchair, the lady walked in. The doctor took one look at the lady and asked what happened. The lady said, "My husband prayed for me, and God healed me." The doctor asked for more blood work: it came back the same as all the others. The lady was healthy. So after a total of forty doctors in three hospitals, God healed.

News and Weather

Years ago, we stopped watching the news on TV. There was a warring conflict going on. One day everything would be calming down; the next day it was heating up and getting worse. Having a family member in the military, you never knew if he was going to have to go or not. So we quit watching the news; it was just too much of an emotional roller-coaster ride—up and going good one day and heading downhill the next. Sometimes it was not even a day; it could all happen in the same day.

And then many years later, a president came out with the saying about fake news. I don't believe that was something new. Just the first time anyone important gave it a name and said something about it. Lots of things are like that. Just regular people know things, it is not believed; but someone with more authority says it, it has to be true.

And now for the weather. You can look out the window and see what the weather is doing. You can listen to the radio or TV to see what the weather is doing or going to do. The only difference is the people on the radio and TV have paid money to go to school to learn to guess about the weather. That is right; I said *guess*. They learn what it is thought the weather will do. But the weather can be unpredictable. It doesn't have to follow any certain pattern or reason for doing what it is doing. Only God knows for sure what the weather will do and when. Everyone else just guesses at it. You say you can put your hand out the window and tell me the weather. You may be able to, and you may not. It can change that fast. Before you get the words out, the weather may change. I have never heard anyone say that the weatherman is putting out fake news.

The internet—if it is on the internet, it must be true. That is what is said, but who is it that puts things on the internet? It is newsmen and others. But do they really know what they are talking about. Is it real news or fake? Do they really know what is true or just repeating what they have heard? Are they adding to it? Are they adding their opinion? I have heard opinions are like armpits—everyone has them, and sometimes they stink. So be careful what you believe. All news may not be real news. Know the source, if you can.

North to Alaska

One family had to travel a lot due to the dad's job. I'm sure there were more moves, but this story is about one. This story is about their trip to and living in Alaska, as if you didn't figure it out by the title. Their trip to Alaska started in North Carolina. The couple had three young children and a dog named Susie. They all piled into their pickup and headed out. The truck had sort of a topper on it; it was almost tall enough to stand up in. And there was a kinda wood box in the front part that covered the second gas tank; they slept on top of it. There was a window in the front of it that connected it to the truck, so some of the kids could crawl back and forth through the window. I say some of them because their ages were six and three years old. There was one more, but he was only six weeks old, too young to crawl yet. They stopped and saw Mount Rushmore and Crazy Horse on the way through. I know that there were another sightseeing stops also; I just can't remember all of them. And of course, there were many bathroom, food, and gas stops. At some of the gas stops, candy was bought for the kids. They would eat the candy and fall asleep instead of being on a sugar high.

The first part of the trip ended in Seattle, Washington. That's where they got on a different kind of highway: the Alaska Marine Highway. That is where you drive your vehicle into the bottom part of the ferry boat. There is a big door that you go through, and above that is more boat. There are lounges, restrooms, places to dine, places to buy food, and cabins to stay in (I don't remember if there was a gift shop or not). You couldn't have any animals up there; they have to stay in the vehicles. But you could go down and take them for walk so they can do their business. This family didn't have a cabin, so they stayed in a lounge. The lounge was just a large room with a lot of large windows and uncomfortable chairs in it (the chairs reclined a bit). The ferry-boat ride was three days long. Three *long* days.

There was one time the captain announced over the speakers that there was a truck that had its brake lights on; they gave the license plate number. It was their truck. The dad knew he hadn't left anything on the pedal, so the lights should not be on. When he got down there, Susie had knocked a briefcase off the seat and onto the brake pedal. When the ride was over, they drove off the boat. They were in Haines, Alaska. There was only a thousand miles left to go. So off they went. They stopped at Haines Junction and gassed up and stretched their legs. It was in the afternoon. Somehow they got turned around and went the wrong way, about a hundred fifty miles the wrong way. So they turned around and went back. When they got going in the right direction, it was late. Everyone but the dad was asleep. Sometime later, the mom woke up and asked if he was going to stop and sleep. He said he would stop when it got dark. She said, "I don't think it's going to get dark. It's one o'clock." So he stopped alongside the road and got some sleep. In the morning, off they went again.

This last part of their trip seemed the longest. That's because there was almost nothing there—well, almost. The road wasn't a nice, smooth paved road; it was a lumpy gravel road. The gravel wasn't small little rocks but fist-sized rocks. Okay, I guess that depends on the fist. In some places, there would be a sign saying that this is going to be the last building for a hundred miles, and it was. There was one time it had snowed, but the road was clear. Well, it started snowing again, and the snow covered everything. I mean *everything*. The kids wanted to stop to play in it, and the mom thought it was beautiful. But the dad didn't like it because he couldn't see where he was going; it was snowing that hard. He wasn't even sure where the road was at times. There was a fence beside the road. He hoped it stayed there because he followed it. That was when he could see it.

Well, they finally made it to Anchorage, Alaska. But they had no home or even knew of a place to go to. They found a motel. It was the Big Timber Motel, right by an airport, a noisy one. The motel didn't allow dogs in the rooms, so Susie had to stay in the truck again. The next morning, the dad went off to find his workplace and let them know that he had arrived. The mom took the kids across the street to a Wendy's. They almost got kicked out because the three-year-old wouldn't stop crying. It disturbed the other people trying to eat. The workers tried giving him a toy, but that didn't help. No one could figure out why he was crying. The family gathered up their food and went back to their room. The mom was already upset. She had thought all their stuff would already be in a house or apartment waiting for them. You see, it was the first of many moves like this one. Fast-forward a little.

They moved into an apartment. It had two stories and a basement. The first floor was the kitchen and living room. The three bedrooms and bathroom were upstairs. The basement was just one big room. One day they were in their apartment unpacking. It was early evening. The two older kids asked if they could go out and play (the youngest one was asleep). The two weren't much help in unpacking, so the dad said yes, but come in when the streetlights come on. That had been the rule in North Carolina, so out they went. Sometime later, the parents were tired and looked at the clock. It was midnight! The kids were still outside playing. The dad called for them to come in. The kids' response was that the lights weren't on yet. The dad's response to that was, "I don't think they will come on."

After a while, they wandered out and found a church they could attend. The weather was different than what they were used to. The summer high was seventy-three degrees one year. One October just before Halloween, it snowed a little bit, just about a foot. I think it was that year the mom was too scared to drive in the snow. She got over that later. So she bundled the kids up and put the two youngest ones in a little red wagon and pulled them to the grocery store; it was only a couple blocks away. The two oldest kids had to walk home; there wasn't any room in the wagon with the food and the youngest one. In the spring, the oldest boy found a cat and brought it home to see if he could keep it—you know how that goes. It was agreed on that he could keep it, so he picked a name for it. The name he picked was Kit the Cat. The cat started marking his territory in the house, so he had to go.

There once was an earthquake while they were home. It scared the oldest child the most. She was on the stairs going down to the basement. The stairs had the wall on one side and nothing on the other side. It wasn't a very big earthquake; it wouldn't have knocked her off the stairs. Everything and everyone were okay; it didn't even knock any pictures off the wall. In the winter, there was a kind of boot called snow boots. The two older kids had them; the youngest one was too small for them. That, however, didn't keep him from wearing his older brother's boots. But he didn't wear them the way they were supposed to be worn. He would put them on his hands and walk around. He had just learned to walk, so there were lots of falls.

The family would go to the park and play and picnic or to a lake to fish. The water was always too cold to swim in. One night it had snowed a foot and a half. So in the morning, mom had to walk in front of the kids and clear a path, no buses to ride, and they don't cancel school. Another time on the way to get the kids from school because they were late, the mom saw a moose coming down the street. A stranger called to her to get in her car. You don't mess with a moose. He had just come from the school where he had gotten his antlers tangled up in a swing's chain. That is why the school didn't let the kids out. When it came time for the family to go back to the lower forty-eight, they had to leave Susie up there. It was sad, but her doctor, a veterinarian, said it would be best for her. They all were sad to leave; they liked it up there. And I think to this day all of them would go back, maybe not to live there but just for a visit.

Ohmm

This is a story about two sisters. The oldest one would climb up on the hood of her grandparents' car, cross her legs, and pretend to meditate. She was so cute with her blonde curly hair just sitting there going, "Ohm…ohm." Many, many years later, the youngest sister was playing with her grandmother on a Sunday afternoon in the living room. The girl lay on her nana's lap, crossed her legs in the air, and said, "Ohm…ohm."

To some of you, this may not be a cute story, but it does have a meaning. You never know what a child will learn or from whom. You see, these two sisters do not get to see each other very much. No one knows where the two ever heard or saw anyone meditate, so where they picked it up at is a mystery.

Both the girls were so cute when they did this. One was sitting upright; the other looked like she had fallen over backward.

Other Mothers

Pick which one fits your situation.
Thank God for your spouse and their parents.

To my other mother,

You are the other mother I received the day I wed your son. And I just want to thank you for the loving things you've done. You've given me a gracious man with whom I share my life. You are his lovely mother and I his lucky wife. You used to pat his little head, and now I hold his hand. You raised in love a little boy and then gave me a man.

To my other mother,

You are the other mother I received the day I wed your daughter. And I just want to thank you for the loving things you've done. You've given me a gracious woman with whom I share my life. You are her lovely mother and I her loving husband. You used to pat her little head, and now I hold her hand. You raised in love a little girl and then gave me a woman.

Ouch

There once was a family of three: the daddy and mommy and a little girl. They lived in a trailer park. It was a nice place to live. It was very quiet and peaceful because it was at the end of town. It was sixteen city blocks from where the dad's parents lived. This is known because the mom walked there once and counted the blocks. One nice summer day, not too hot of a day, the windows were opened to let some fresh air in. Dad went to work as he always did. Mom and their daughter were at home. Mom was in the kitchen doing the breakfast dishes. The little girl was playing in the living room. Mom would look and check on her every now and again. The last time she checked on her, she was standing in the chair just looking out the window. There was a big tree on the other side of the porch and, just past that, a small pond.

The mom heard crying coming from outside. Her daughter had climbed up into the window and pushed the screen out. She had fallen out the window onto a concrete slab porch. It was about a six-foot drop. The little girl must have landed on her head because there was a lump the size of a goose egg on one side of her forehead. The mom knew that there was a chance her daughter might have a concussion. It was said not to let a person with a concussion go to sleep. The little girl wanted to go to sleep. Mom had no way to get to a doctor; dad had taken the only car they had to work.

Mom got scared and called her mother-in-law. She was the relative that lived the closet to them. When she got there, they headed to the emergency room. On the way there, the girl threw up all over her mom. That was a sign of a concussion. They both were worried. The doctor said that there wasn't a concussion. Kids wanted to go to sleep to get away from the pain, and the girl threw up because of all the crying she had done. The doctor said it would be all right to let the girl sleep, but try waking her up about every hour to make sure she would wake up. And then they were sent home. When dad got home, mom had to tell him all about the day. He could tell something had happened because the lump was still on his daughter's head. As far as they could tell, there was no permanent damage—to the girl or the concrete porch. And of course, the chair was moved away from the window. There was maybe a side effect from the fall: the girl, now grown, is afraid of heights.

Painting, Painting, Painting

A family decided to paint their downstairs bathroom. It had a walk-in shower, sink, and toilet in it. It was a small bathroom. The three kids wanted to help. The parents said they thought it would be okay. Good experience for the kids. The walls were readied for painting; the paint supplies were obtained. The time had come to paint. The kids, all three of them, did some of the painting. Can't say for sure how they all fit in there at once. The kids did what might be called a kid paint job. They didn't get enough paint on the roller, so the old paint could still be seen through the new in places. The dad then painted the bathroom again while the kids weren't home. He didn't want to hurt their feelings. Mom said she could see roller marks in the paint, so she was told she should have painted it herself. The mom then painted the bathroom again. All this took several days to accomplish. Each layer of paint had to dry before it could be painted over. You know that it was a small bathroom because it took less than a gallon of paint.

This story came to my mind because at this time, my husband and myself are in the process of redoing our downstairs bathroom. I get to be the only one who will be painting. The kids are all grown up and have moved out. They can paint their own bathrooms. Hopefully, they do a better job than they did when they were young. That is unless they are going for an abstract-art look. I really don't think abstract art belongs in a bathroom.

Pass Around Kids

There once was a couple. They had three kids. The word *kids* in this story refers to "children." The dad's job included a lot of time away from his family. Sometimes he would be gone for a few days, and sometimes it would be for weeks or even months at a time. There was this one time he was going to be gone for a whole year. Well, about halfway through the year, he found out that he could come home for a little while. So he got the idea that maybe his wife could come over and visit him before he went home for a visit. So the family made a plan. The mom would go visit the dad, and then the dad would come home with her and visit with the kids and family. There was a small problem. The kids weren't the problem; it was who would take care of them. They couldn't go with their mom, and none of their aunts, uncles, or grandparents could take care of them for that long a period. It was only going to be a week or two. So they all came up with a plan and a schedule: the kids would stay with each of their relatives for a few days. They were passed around from family to family. But the kids enjoyed it. They got to visit with their aunts, uncles, cousins, and grandparents for a little while. And then when the mom was to come home, the dad would be with her, and then the kids could go back home. The family was together again for a little while, and then the dad was off again. His family was sad he had to go, but they were used to it; it was part of his job. The dad didn't like it either, but he knew he had to go to provide for his family and his job required it. He did what a dad is supposed to do: provide for his family.

Pets

Over the years, it seems like my families have always had a cat or a dog or both, sometimes more than one of each kind of animal. By "families," I mean the one I had growing up, and the other is the one I started when I got married. Oh, I almost forgot about the hamsters and gerbils; and of course, what family at some time or another hasn't had a fish bowl, tank, or pond?

Let me tell you about some of the pets. There was a cat named Two Eyes. Yes, most cats do have two eyes, but this one had a blue eye and a green eye. And he was deaf also. He was an all-white cat, except for his eyes. I don't remember if his mother was Crybaby or Snow. Those two were sisters, and they both were all white. And it seemed like they always had kittens at the same time. There was one time Two Eyes was asleep in the kitchen, and my future husband was going to pet him. Instead, he must have scared him, so the cat bit the hand that petted him.

After we got married, we lived in a very small apartment, so we didn't take the two-eyed cats with us. Since I was raised with cats and dogs around all the time, I got lonely when my new husband went to work. He got me a kitten named Tonto to keep me company. I don't remember why we didn't have him for long. Some pets were around a long time and others a short time. A person can get really attached to a pet. Some pets have life better than some people.

One day I was on my way to visit with my mom and had a wreck. I totaled the car my husband and I had just got. I felt so bad about it that I was given a dog named Terry to make me feel better. As I was carrying the groceries in one day, she kept getting in the way and almost tripped me. I picked her up and tossed her out of the way. She landed on the grass but must have landed the wrong way: she broke her leg. She healed just fine, and one day a while after that, she had some puppies. One was named Speck (we gave him to my husband's parents), and he has a story of his own.

There have been many other pets, some with names and some without. There have been many fish in tanks, bowls, and/or ponds, and even some eels. Eels are hard to keep in a tank. Somehow they kept getting out, and then when they are found, they are all dried up lying on the carpet. Buck! Most of the fish didn't have names, but there was a goldfish that somehow got the name *Um*. He lived in a tank, and the cat we had at that time would get himself a drink of water out of the tank. It was quite funny to watch. As the cat drank, the fish would sink to the bottom and look up at the cat. There were a couple of hamsters. They were called Pete and Puff. They were supposed to live in an aquarium—without water, of course. Almost every day they seemed to get out. Most of the time it was at night. Someone would be awakened by them making noises. Many years after them, one of the kids got some gerbils. They were given the names Rambo and Rambo the Second. They were also hard to keep in their cage.

Most of the time, the kids got to name the pets. There was a dog named Ruff; another one was called Tippy. Not hard to figure out why. There was also a cat named Kit the Cat. Most of the time, the name described the pet; sometimes it didn't. Can you figure out what kind of animal a Herb or an Ivan would be? There was also a Buster, Susie, Missy, Garfield, Patches, and many others over the years. Most of the pets have a little story about them that someone in the family remembers. What fun it is to talk with one another and recall the stories.

Playing with a Doughnut

There once was an odd family. I will tell you about one odd thing they did. Maybe not odd but strange. There was this one time when four generations of them got together. There was a great-grandmother, a grandmother, a mother, and her two girls. They all wanted to do something together. But you see, the great-grandmother's health was not that good, so it was difficult to think of something. Somehow one of them came up with the idea to throw a chocolate-covered doughnut back and forth to one another. Doesn't that sound messy? This was in the living room. This doughnut was not a regular doughnut; this doughnut was a sponge. They thought it might have been a dog toy but weren't sure if it was or not. They weren't even sure where it came from. But that didn't matter or stop them. Well, anyway, they threw it back and forth to one another, or should I say *at* one another. Some of the throws had a lot of force behind them. Nothing got broken (believe me, there were plenty of things on the tables and walls to break).

They all laughed and laughed. They had a ball that day—or would that be they all had a *doughnut* that day? It doesn't matter; they all enjoyed it. It was not just the playing together but being together that mattered.

Protection

There are all kinds of protection. Some people say their insurance provides them protection. Others say there is a protection better and greater than that. It is God. Some people know for sure God is protecting them. Late one night while sleeping, the lady of the house was woken up by a loud noise. She wasn't sure what it was. She wasn't worried about it. She rolled over and went back to sleep. In the morning, she found out there had been a tornado in the area. No damage to their property. There was a path of ripped-up trees across the street and in the woods behind their house. Her husband wasn't home that night; he was on a field trip. That means going to the woods and doing things. That is part of army life. Sleeping in the cab of a truck, he was woken up by the moving of the truck. He wasn't worried; he just put the truck in neutral to see if it would go anywhere.

Over the years, neighbors on both sides of their house have had the roofs replaced due to storm damage. Yes, their insurance provided protection from financial loss. Better than that is the protection God provided. The storms did no damage to the house in the middle. Other storms tore trees in half across the street from the house, but again no damage, not even a lawn chair knocked over. There was one storm that uprooted a big oak tree in the neighbor's yard. When it fell, it knocked over another oak tree and several cedar trees. These weren't small trees. One oak tree fell into the woods, and the other tree fell on a fence between the two houses. As they fell, they took out the power lines. All three houses were without power for a while, and so were a lot of other people in the state. The family in the middle only received damage to the fence. It cost them about twelve dollars to fix it. *Wow*, what protection they have! They also got a lot of firewood for themselves and others in their church. One of their friends with a sawmill got the cedar trees. What a good deal for all of them—wood without having to cut a tree down.

The protection isn't just on a house while they are at home. God also took care of them in the car. At a busy intersection when they started to turn on a green-turn arrow, the car in the oncoming traffic ran a red light and hit their car. No one was hurt, just a little damage to the car.

A young man moved out of his parents' house to a different state, and his protector went with him. God can be in more than one place at a time. While the man was on his way to work one morning, he was in an accident. He was driving on a highway, and a car turned in front of him. He didn't have time to react before the two autos collided. His emergency brake pedal was driven into his left calf. He was extracted from his truck, and then he was life-flighted to a hospital with a trauma unit. It wasn't the nearest hospital but the best one. No head injury, and his chest wasn't crushed by the steering wheel. His seat and steering wheel only had about six inches between them. The truck didn't have airbags. That would have been worse. He did receive a broken left arm and of course some damage to his left leg. He was only out of work for a short time. *Wow!*

There was another young man who went canoeing with a friend. They both were good swimmers. They both wore their life jackets. One canoe turned over, and the young man was held under the water by the current. He somehow was able to come to the top of the water. He was okay, close call. Now tell me that God wasn't protecting this family and young men better than any insurance could. Some may call it luck. Some may call it a coincidence. Some *do* say it is God providing the protection.

Raiding the Closet

There once was a girl who would go and visit with her grandparents. Her grandparents thought that was so sweet since she was in college. They all lived in the same town, not far apart. Her grandparents weren't as dumb as the granddaughter thought they were. Because when the grandparents went to the store, they would always buy a few extra things that the granddaughter liked. So when the granddaughter came to visit, she always looked in the fridge and pantry to see what good things there were to eat. The pantry was just some shelves behind bifold doors. There was always something good to eat; the grandparents both were good cooks. And sometimes the girl would even ask to take some of the goodies home or to school with her. And that was okay because that was why the grandparents bought the extra stuff in the first place, so she could take some of it. They didn't know if the granddaughter knew extras were bought with her in mind or not.

This is one way the grandparents showed they loved and cared for the granddaughter and anyone else who might need food. You see, they have shared with others in need. This is a way of sharing God's love with others.

Retired or Not

Some people ask, "What will I do with my spare time when I retire?" But you might not have any spare time. You might fill it with things you have wanted to do for a while or even wanted to do for a long time, or others might fill it for you. There is also traveling and sightseeing, getting together with friends and family, camping, hunting and fishing, and even going on mission trips. There is a long list of things a person could come up with to do. Take some time to do this even if you are not retired. Some people call it a bucket list.

But I have found that writing these stories is very relaxing and enjoyable—just to sit and remember what all has gone on in the past. Or I write stories that come to my mind, or I make up something. I have also found that when you are hunting or fishing and get nothing, that can be good. Let me explain. Let's say you are deer hunting; most people sit in a blind or tree stand. A blind can be like a little tent with a lot of windows; usually there are two people in it. A tree stand is where you climb a small ladder and sit on a platform in a tree. You are supposed to be strapped in so you don't fall out. Yeah, it is good if you see an animal that you are hunting and get to shoot at it.

But there is so much more that can be done. You can just sit and watch the birds, squirrels, and other animals. Or you can just sit and listen to all of nature. You can watch the clouds go by or find shapes in them as you might have done as a child. You don't have to hunt to do this; you can do it in your backyard or even on a picnic or walk. You could take the kids or grandkids; enjoy the time with them. You could also look at all the things God has made for us. Thank God for it all. Talk with Him, or you can sit and wait for Him to talk to you.

You can admire the sky, grass, trees, clouds, animals, and be thankful for them. So take some time to just sit and look around you—you don't have to be retired to do that. You can make time for whatever you think is important. So take some time to just sit and enjoy your life. Don't fill it with a lot of stupid stuff. Also get up and go, for you may not be able to later.

Oh, camping and fishing are also a very good time to just sit back and enjoy what God has made. You know, He made it for everyone. So enjoy. I have found that even a person who likes to stay inside can enjoy the beauty God has made. All you have to do is look out the window. Sometimes I will be sitting in a chair looking out the window, and my husband will ask what I am doing. I tell him I am watching the trees grow. I do not really see the trees growing. I'm just enjoying looking outside while staying warm and dry inside. So don't forget to enjoy life, no matter what is going on in your life. You are not promised any tomorrows.

Shells and Smells

There was a couple who went to visit their son and his wife and their boys. The two couples lived in two different states. They all enjoyed their time together when they were able to get together. When they got together, the boys asked, "Are you taking us out for ice cream?" The grandparents loved it when the boys asked that question. One reason was that it meant that there was ice cream in the near future. On to the shells and smells.

One evening, they all went to the beach and wadded in the bay. The water was a little chilly. While there on the beach, Nana picked up what she thought were empty shells. They all enjoyed their time together. But the visit came to an end, as all visits do. It was a sad time for both families. Nana and Papaw left and headed home. When they got home, they unloaded the car. They went on with their lives as usual. A couple days later, they noticed a strange smell in the car. A couple more days passed, and the smell got even worse. So they searched the car for the cause of the smell. All they found were the shells that had been collected. They had been left them in the car; they were rolled up in a sun bonnet Nana kept in the car. So they removed the shells from the car, but the smell kept getting worse and worse anyway. They searched the car again. This time, they found the cause of the smell. One of the shells hadn't been empty: it had a hermit crab living in it. It had crawled up under the floor mat and died. They removed it from the car and let the car air out.

Weeks went by, but the smell didn't go away. So they traded the car in for a new one. Oh, they might have traded it in anyway; we don't know for sure. But they both enjoyed the new odorless car—and always made sure all the shells picked up after that were empty, wrapped in plastic, and taken out of the car when they got home.

Shyness

There once was a couple who had a little baby girl. She was a cute little girl, and now she is a cute big girl. Her Nana and Papaw didn't live close to her and her family. The families lived in two different states, with a state in between them. They all loved one another and would go and visit one another when they could. When the baby got big enough to sit on the couch or someone's lap to play, she didn't want anything to do with her grandparents. Her daddy said she was that shy with everyone, not just them. She didn't know them. You can't blame her. After she had grown some, she was even so shy she wouldn't hug them goodbye; she wouldn't even hug them with her daddy holding her. I think she was and still is a daddy's girl. Well, after several years went by, she wasn't as shy. I don't know if she grew out of it or just got more used to the grandparents. She would give her Nana a little hug. But she wouldn't hug her Papaw. She would, however, give him a high five. And he was glad she did. He didn't want her to be forced to love him.

Sledding

Do you know how to go sledding without any snow? Let me tell you about how it came about. A dad took his children sledding one warm, sunny fall day. There were no coats or gloves needed, and they used only cardboard boxes as sleds. The boxes didn't even get soggy because there was no snow. The dad and kids walked up a small hill to a shady spot under some pine trees.

They put the cardboard boxes down flat and climbed on top. With the kids one behind the other, there came just a little push, and away they went down the hill, sledding on the pine needles. Taking turns sledding and pushing, they all had a great time; they did this for hours. The kids and dad had so much fun that day. And to this day, they all talk about it being one of the funniest days of their lives. They say it was more fun than if they would have sledded on snow. They didn't have to stop and warm up.

So if you have not tried it, you should. Having fun with the kids doesn't have to be a big expense, unless you want it to be. Use your imagination. See what you and the kids can come up with. Enjoy your time together. Kids grow up so fast, and if you do things together, you will know them better.

God gives us kids to raise, not to let them raise themselves or to let electronics raise them. So spend time with the kids. You say the day is not long enough or you don't have time. You can make time for whatever is important enough. Skip the internet; spend that time with the kids. You will make better memories that way.

Just remember back to when you were a kid and improve on that. How could you improve the time you spent with your parents? Make memories today. We are not promised tomorrow.

Snowflakes and People

Two totally different things but, in a way, the same. If you think about snowflakes, they say that no two are alike. Out of who knows how many snowflakes there have been in the past and future, no two have or will look alike. Do you have the imagination or memory to do that? God does. Then there is the way that they come down. Sometimes the flakes just seem to slowly drift down from the sky like a feather. At other times, they come down like they weigh a ton, falling hard and fast. It has been said that in the center of each snowflake there is a speck of dirt or dust surrounded by the beautiful flake part.

People are the same in a way. Let's look at people. I don't think any two are alike. Not even twins. Oh, a set of twins may look almost alike, but not exactly alike. There may be a mole or birthmark that could be different, or their personalities may be different. Do you have the imagination or memory to make each person different? God does. Then there is the way they go through life. Some people just seem to glide through life with no problems. Others seem to always be struggling, having a hard time. But in the center of each person is the same red blood that flows through their veins. Each one is different on the outside but the same on the inside.

God made each person different. It was not to have those differences held against us. We should not treat people badly just because their skin or language is different from ours. God takes the time to make each and every snowflake and person different. He loves each person the same, no matter how different they may be. He has a plan for each person's life. If life seems to be messed up, you can change it. Snowflakes melt and change; we can change also. But be careful. Some changes or choices may make life worse. I have heard it said that God doesn't make junk. So if there ain't no junk people, then we all are worth something. That is why God sent His Son, Jesus, to the earth to die for us. Think about it. God must really love everyone who was and is to come.

Some Mornings

There was a single mom raising two girls. She was doing this with her parents' help. Being single, the mom had to work to provide for her family. This story is about the youngest girl. Since Mom had to be at work early in the morning on some school days, she would take her youngest girl to the grandparents' house. That's where the bus would pick the little girl up at. After breakfast, the little girl and her grandma would go out to watch for the bus. Some mornings, they had time to play. Some mornings they would play tag. The little girl liked running around and around the car and truck. Some mornings they would play hide-and-seek. This was hard to do because there were no good places to hide. The grandma would hide behind a tree, but it was not a big tree, or she held the little girl's backpack up to her head and hide behind it. They had to hide where they could and watch for the bus also.

Some mornings they would play "Look out!" That was something the little girl had made up. She would ride her blade, which is just a skinny scooter. She would head straight for her grandma. When they were close, the little girl would yell, "Look out!" The grandma then would act frightened and get out of the way before she was run into or over. Some mornings they would sit on the front porch and play with some small plastic yard ornaments. There were squirrels, rabbits, and chipmunks to play with. They would pretend the animals could talk and move. For some reason, there was always a mean animal (the grandma was always the mean one). Some mornings they would pretend that the driveway was lava. The little girl would yell, "Hot lava!" Then they both would run off the driveway into the grass before they got burned up.

Some mornings they would sit in lawn chairs in the driveway and pretend to watch TV. Some mornings they would pretend that the little girl was a police officer and the grandma was a bad guy. She then would be caught and put in jail. The grandma would be worn out by the time the bus came, but she enjoyed the time with her granddaughter. Some mornings the little girl's grandpa would sit on the back of the car and watch them play. He enjoyed watching them play. Some mornings the little girl didn't come over and catch the bus. On those mornings, she was missed by her grandparents.

Somebody Is in Trouble

You arrive home after a long day of work, and the house is quiet. This is not normal because you have three teenagers all living at home. As you go past the door, you notice a dead silence. As you go through the kitchen into the living room, there sit all three teenagers on the couch, just as quiet as can be. Their hands are on their laps. They are sitting up straight, both feet on the floor—what a sight. Are they at home or the principal's office? You ask where their mother is. They softly whisper, "Upstairs. She's mad." You ask, "Is she mad at me? And how do you know she is mad?" The answer is, "She is mad at us. She said the D word." You know she had to be really mad to say something like that. She never says anything like that. You go upstairs, and there she is, sitting on the bed. You think you see something coming from her collar. Is it smoke, or is it steam? After a little while, everyone gets over it, whatever it was. The house is noisy and full of activity again as usual. No one even remembers what made her that mad or which child or children it was.

And if anyone does remember, they are not telling.

Taking Over

This is about a very nice family. I have to tell you about the family before I tell you about the taking over. There was the dad, mom, daughter, and two sons. As the children grew, the family moved from place to place. They were never in one place for more than three years or so. With all the moving and traveling, the kids got to see all kinds of places, and they even got to travel to others countries. So with all that moving, the kids didn't really have a room to call their own or were able to decorate the way they wanted. The last move the family made, they were going to stay there for at least six years—oh, what a joy to stay in one place for that long.

The house they lived in had three bedrooms. The master bedroom and a girls' room, and of course the other one was called the boys' room. The family lived there more than six years. One of the boys painted the walls in the boys' room. He painted life-size comic-book characters. There was a Spawn, Batman, and a Spiderman. He was the artist of the family. The parents continued to live there even after the kids had all grown and moved out. Spawn was painted over; he was creepy. Batman and Spiderman still remain on the wall. The boys both moved to different states after graduating high school.

The oldest son moved to the parents' hometown. His parents were from the same town. Once he got there, he moved in with his grandparents. Then he found a good job. He then moved into an apartment of his own. Then he met a girl, dated her for a while, then married her. They got themselves a house of their own to live in. Then they started their own family. They had a little girl.

The youngest son joined the military, and of course, he moved to wherever he was sent. And then he met a young lady, dated her, then they got married. They found a place of their own to call their home. The young lady had two boys, so the young man instantly had a family of his own.

Now on to the daughter. She graduated high school. She had a job before she graduated. She found herself a guy, dated him, and married him. Her husband was in the military, so they lived wherever he was stationed. They started a family of their own. They had a little girl. The marriage didn't last. After a while, the daughter married again. Then they started a family of their own. They had a little girl. The marriage didn't last.

On to the taking-over part. The two bedrooms had always been referred to as the boys' room and the girls' room. Now the daughter had to have a job to provide for her two daughters. The grandparents watched the oldest daughter till she was grown. Her younger sister was twelve years younger than her. The grandparents took care of her also. Sometimes the youngest granddaughter would have to spend the night with her grandparents while the mom worked. She would always want to sleep in the boys' room. At some time, she started calling it her room. So the girls' room stayed the girls' room. The boys' room, however, is now called by two different names. Sometimes it is still called the boys' room, and sometimes it's called Abby's room. It shouldn't matter what it's called; it still is a bedroom. It has the same beds the boys slept in. Some of the boys' toys are still in the room—and they still get played with.

Taking Pictures

There once was a very young girl. She was probably about one and a half years old. She had a play camera she liked playing with. She loved to take pictures. She would also get into trouble taking pictures when she used her parents' Instamatic camera. That was a camera way back in time. All you had to do was push a button, and it spat a picture out. Well, almost. You would have to wait for a few minutes for the picture to develop right before your eyes. The young girl would climb up on the bar between the living room and the kitchen and take pictures. She took many pictures of her feet and her belly. I guess that was her form of selfie.

One day her parents took her somewhere in the truck. That was the family car. She was alone in the pickup truck for just a little while with the camera. Her parents were close by, but not close enough to stop her from taking several pictures. She took pictures of the dash and the floor. And so her parents learned not to leave the camera out where the young girl could reach it or climb up to get it or even find it. I don't think the girl even owns a camera now. It's amazing what all a phone can do.

Tea Parties

Have you ever seen a fancy tea party on TV or in a movie? Well, I did, and I thought it would be nice to go to one or have one. So one day I sat down and planned one out. What shall I serve? When should I have it? How long will it last? When I had it all figured out, I had the party. Oh, the "what to serve" was the hardest part. As I recall, it was on a Saturday (don't remember the date or time, however). I sent out invitations to all of our daughters and their girls. I really didn't expect two of them and their daughters to make it; they live in other states. That would have been a long way to go for tea. Well, the family that did show up had a great time. We all had tea or hot chocolate to drink (the little ones don't like tea). And we had lots of goodies to eat. Our waiter did a very good job. No tips for him, except he got to eat the leftovers. You see, I had my husband as the waiter; and as I said, he did a very good job. We all had a great time, even the little ones. Everyone drank and ate all the food and goodies they wanted.

Each one who attended received a gift; the ones who didn't make it got their gift at a later time. The gift was their very own teapot and cup, picked out with each person in mind. There were lots of pictures taken. Then the photos were printed and put in photo albums and given to my daughters; they had to share with their girls. The tea party went over so well I plan on having several more. And as far as I can tell, everyone enjoyed themselves.

Technology

Some people say it is wonderful. I only like parts of it. I got a new computer in February. I had to learn or be shown how to use it. It was different from the tablet and notebook I had been using. Well, just the other day, my new computer would not let me do anything on it. This is only March; it should not break yet. I called my tech support, and she came over to look at it. It is nice to have smart children living close by. There was nothing wrong with the computer. The trial period for using the writing part had run out. I thought as long as I was able to type, things would keep working. Not so. So she got me going again. Then everything I wrote was put in an open file, or so I thought. Tech support again. This time, she said I misunderstood what the computer was saying. Yes, the computer talks. It didn't actually say in a voice you could hear that my stuff was in an open file. That is what it printed behind the file. But back to the talking part, the computer can really talk. When I first got it, she said her name was Cortana. That has been the only time she has talked to me. The computer has to have internet connection for her to be able to talk. I am sure that there is other technology out there that is just as confusing to others, not just us older folks.

 Think about TV. It used to be that you just plugged them in and turned them on, no big mess of cables going everywhere. No sound system to hook up. No VCR or DVD or Blu-ray players to hook up, just maybe an antenna. And that is so you could get four or five channels, not like the hundreds that are out there now. But having more channels doesn't mean that there is anything worth watching going to be on. It was the same way with the four or five channels. The good part about technology is you can watch one program and record or save another to watch later. Before, you would just have to miss one of the programs.

A good thing about all this is the advances it has made in the medical field. The advances in medicines and in surgeries, and the tests doctors can do to find out what is going on in a person's body. The doctors no longer have to just guess at what is wrong, or so I hope. There was one time I was ill and saw forty-six doctors in three different hospitals, and they all said if or when I found out what was wrong, to let them know. That was twenty-three years ago, so hopefully there have been some advances. That is just in case it would happen again.

The Cowgirl

There once was a beautiful little girl. She liked dressing up like a cowgirl. When she went to her Nana and Papaw's house, she would ride their horse. She would dress in her blue jeans and have her gun belt on. It held two six-shooters. She also had her Stetson hat sitting cockeyed on her head. There was beautiful long brown hair flowing down her back. She climbed upon the beautiful horse. She called it her trustee steed. The horse was a beautiful brown-and-white rocking horse named *Grandma*. After riding for a while—or shall we say *rocking* for a while—do you know what she did? Without even blinking an eye, the beautiful little cowgirl slowly pulled out one of her guns and pointed it at her Nana. Nana pretended she was frightened. The little cowgirl then demanded, "Put up your hands!" Nana put up her hands slowly as she was demanded to do. And then without any warning at all, Nana was shot. The young cowgirl was a very good shot. It only took one shot to get her Nana. The cowgirl then told her Nana, "You're dead." And then with that being done, the little cowgirl put her gun in the holster and continued to ride Grandma the horse. It wasn't off into the sunset as in most stories and movies; Grandma can't go that far.

The Crisco Kid

There once was a wee little boy. This boy and his family were watching TV in the living room one evening (or at least that is what they thought), but the little boy had slipped away. The family noticed that he was missing after a little bit. There was a discussion on who would go look for him. The mom got up to look for him. He was being too quiet. They all thought he must be up or into something or asleep somewhere. Mom went to the kitchen, and there he was. He really was into something. He had been caught being a slick kid. I mean a really slick kid. He had gotten into the cabinet under the kitchen sink—I mean he *really* got into the cabinet, so far in he only had one leg hanging out. Under the sink, he had found a thirty-two-ounce bottle of Crisco oil and opened it. Then he poured it out on himself and had a puddle on the floor by his foot. Mom called for dad to come see what his son had done. She then asked him if he wanted to clean the floor or the boy. You know that they both had to be scrubbed and cleaned. What a slippery mess. The dad picked the floor to clean, so the slick boy was taken by his mom and scrubbed up. After that, the oil was kept in a higher place, a place where he couldn't get it. No one wanted another oil spill like that.

The Flight

There was a couple who had three children. The father had a job that involved a lot of travel. There was one time that his job took him to Germany, and the family could go too, but not at the same time. So the family all planned their trip. His job sent him to Germany a few months before his family. They all thought at first it was to find them a home. But that didn't happen. His job had him going from one place to another. Then it came time for the rest of the family to go over there. The ages of the kids were three, six, and nine years old at that time. So the family got ready to go over there. The mom went and found the biggest suitcases she could find; she bought two of them. Well, when she packed them, they each weighed about 110 pounds. The Castle Grayskull the youngest child had wouldn't fit, so they took it on the plane as a carry-on. It was the first long flight any of them had taken.

There was a four-hour layover in New York City, New York. They stayed in the airport, afraid they might get lost and miss their plane. Also they had heard some stories about how bad the city was. The prices were high. They had to pay a lot just to eat hot dogs; things were expensive there. Well, when they got on another plane, the youngest and oldest both said they didn't feel well. But the middle child was fine. So when they got to Germany where the dad was, he said, "Take them to the doctor." Off they went to the doctor in the morning.

The oldest one had the chicken pox; the youngest one had a bad tooth. So the oldest was confined to her room, no going out to eat, because they had no way to fix food. The youngest had to have a root canal done. The dentist said it wouldn't be too painful for him. The dentist had mom sit in the chair with him on her lap and hold him still. Believe me, it was bad. It did hurt a lot; it hurt both of them. Since they had no house yet, they stayed in what was called a guesthouse. That is a place that has a lot of rooms for people to stay who are coming or going. They had two bedrooms with a bathroom in the middle, hooking them together. Kinda like a hotel but different. And when the cleaning lady came to clean the room and change the sheets, mom had to try to explain about the chicken pox to her. That wasn't easy because the cleaning lady didn't speak any English, and the mom didn't speak any German. Of course, the oldest child shared the chicken pox with the middle child, so he was sick two weeks later. Then the middle child shared them with his younger brother, and he was sick two weeks after that. The mom got to take care of all of them because the dad couldn't get close to his children. You see, he had never had the chicken pox and didn't want to catch them either. And he didn't.

The Giraffe and the Rabbit

One day there was a giraffe in the deep dark jungle eating some yummy green leaves from the top of a tree. He thought they tasted good. He was so sad because he wanted to eat some of the beautiful green grass way down below him on the ground. But his legs were too long, he couldn't get his head down far enough to reach the beautiful green grass. He was tired of always having to eat only the leaves from the tops of the trees. While he was standing there feeling sorry for himself, along came a rabbit, eating some of the beautiful green grass. But he was sad too. He was tired of always having to eat only the green grass. He wished he could eat some of the beautiful green leaves way up high in the tops of the trees. But he couldn't. He was to small and too short to reach any of the leaves.

The giraffe got to talking with the rabbit, and they told each other their problems. That got them to thinking, and they came up with an idea. The giraffe would drop some of the leaves from the top of the trees, and then the rabbit would be able to eat them. This made the rabbit very happy. And if the rabbit were to dig four deep holes in the ground, the giraffe could put a foot into each of the holes; then he would be able to reach and eat some of the grass. Well, that's just what they did. And each one was so very happy. They had worked together and helped each other solve their problems. It is a good thing to help others. It makes you feel good. They became the very best of friends after that. They continued to help each other; that is what friends do.

The Old—or Shall We Say Older—Couple

I always wondered why I found a score sheet on the kitchen table when I visited my parents. They had played many card games together at the table. You see, they both were retired and spent most of their time at home. I guess they couldn't find much of anything else to do.

I now understand why the score sheet was there. You see, I'm now part of a retired couple who spends a lot of time at home together. Sometimes we will sit around asking each other, "What do you want to do?" and the answer to that is, "I don't know. What do *you* want to do?" Other times we play cards. We have played many Russian rummy games, and Uno games, and many, many games of War. And sometimes if the other person is not there or is busy, it may be solitaire. For you younger ones, those are the names of some card games that are played with cards you have to hold in your hand, not on a phone.

We also sit on the swing and watch the fish swim and splash around in the fish pond. We also watch the plastic duck move around on the water. We sometimes see a snake doctor, or some may call them dragonflies. We watch the birds flying around and eating from the bird feeder and the squirrels doing what squirrels do. Sometimes we even see hummingbirds. Ahh, on a cloudy night, we sit and watch the lighting bugs flying all around. Some of you may know them as fireflies. We also watch the traffic going up and down the road. Sounds exciting, doesn't it? Sometimes we even watch movies and old TV series. Those are the ones we put in the VCR or DVD player. We don't have cable or satellite or a dish or internet or any fancy hooptie like that. And even if it is or sounds boring, I would like many more years of that. I would also like for our children, grandchildren, great-grandchildren, and so on down the line to do the same. I hope whoever reads this gets to experience this also. It may sound boring, but it's very relaxing. You can do what you want to do. Just enjoy your life. Take time to relax and unwind.

The Three Little Kids

Oh, don't be fooled. The word *kids* in this story refers to "children." There were two boys and one girl. The girl was the oldest. One day the girl and her oldest brother were playing with some lock blocks or Legos, whatever you want to call them. They were trying to build something (you know how kids are). But the youngest brother kept bothering them (isn't that what little brothers do?). He kept knocking their blocks apart. Now the youngest brother was so young he could not even walk yet. So his brother and sister went and sat on the stair landing; there were three stairs below that. They thought they would be safe there. The youngest one could not climb the stairs yet. So he pulled himself up and stood and watched his brother and sister playing. And of course, he fussed at them, but it was in baby talk, so no one knew what he was really saying. It didn't bother his brother and sister to hear him fuss; they didn't pay any attention to him. Isn't that what brothers and sisters do?

Valuables

There are many different things people value, or think are valuable, that can't be replaced. Some women value their jewelry. Some women value their furs. Some people value their car, truck, or maybe a boat. Others may value their art pieces. To value something means to think it's worth a lot or to think it can't be replaced because it means a lot to you.

I have jewelry that is valuable. I don't, at this time have, any furs and don't care if I ever have any. There are some art pieces in the house that may be worth something. But it all can be replaced. That's what insurance is for, right? I can think of other things I have that are valuable to me and that can't be replaced. My God is the first and then my family. I have some jewelry my son made for me. There's this one piece made from the spring of an ink pen. It is stretched out and has some precious jewels on it; they are precious because they were glued to the spring by my son. It was made into a necklace for me. How do you replace something like that? There are also many pieces of art. That is the art my kids and grandkids have made for me over the years. You say, what about the photos you have collected over the years? Some may have copies out there somewhere, which we could have made more copies of. That doesn't matter to much. I still have my family, and we could have more pictures taken.

You see, I also have some memories trapped in my head. Those are valuable; you can't replace them. Friends are also very valuable and can't be replaced. Oh yeah, you can make new friends, but they're not the same as the other ones you had before. So hang on to some stuff if you want, but make sure you build memories with your family and friends. Take a walk, fly a kite, have a picnic, just do something together. Get out and enjoy your life, family, and friends before it's too late.

Vines

As a young girl, I remember going to my grandparents' house for a visit. We didn't live very close to each other, so we didn't go very often. They had an old farm with a house, barn, corncrib, smokehouse, chicken house, and an outhouse. Someone may have to explain to the young ones what all these houses are—that is, if they know themselves. There were apple trees growing behind the smokehouse and red plum trees and grapevines between the barn and house. Up the hill on the other side of the house was a big strawberry patch. Believe me, none of the fruit went to waste.

There were times when we went to visit and got to help pick up the apples and plums that had fallen on the ground. They were made into pies, fritters, jams, jellies, and other good things. We also would walk up the hill to pick strawberries, The strawberries were good, but I didn't like going up the hill carrying baskets or buckets to put the berries in; those are the ones that we didn't eat.

Years later, the house and barn had to be torn down because they were falling down. The grapevines were going to be bulldozed down to make way for a mobile home to be put up. My mom dug up some of the vines and took them home. She remembered picking grapes off the vines when she was young, so for many years, there were grapevines at my house. Many years later, no one had been keeping the weeds from growing up in the vines. It became almost impossible to pick the grapes. With many years of neglect, the vines started to get chocked out by weeds. Many years later again, my husband and I thought we would do something about that. So on one of our trips to visit my parents, we went out and dug up what vines we could find. There wasn't but a few. Now we have grapevines growing in our backyard. The vines are doing well and producing many grapes. I think the birds eat more grapes than I pick, but that is okay. I just like having the vines because of their history. They still are made into jelly.

Our daughter knows the story of the vines, and she wants the vines if we ever decide to get rid of them or we move and don't want to take them with us. I think, with love and care, the grapevines will outlive all of us. Just like us, plants need someone to care for and take care of them.

Visions

There once was a family: the dad, mom, and two children. The dad's job took him away from his family a lot. This time, he had to go for some schooling and would be gone through Thanksgiving. The mom and children went to stay with her parents while he would be gone. Only the couple and their parents knew that there was another child on the way. Oh, don't worry, I will get to the vision part. There was a four-day weekend for Thanksgiving at the dad's school. He decided to go and spend the time with his family. They all had an enjoyable Thanksgiving. The mom didn't want to worry the dad, so she didn't tell him that there had been complications with the pregnancy. She didn't want to worry him; he couldn't do anything but worry. And believe me, he was and is still good at worrying. Well, things took a turn for the worse the Friday after Thanksgiving. The mom was taken by ambulance to the hospital: she had a miscarriage. She had to be in the hospital a few days. The dad had to leave for school while she was still in the hospital. He didn't want to go. He felt bad about it, but he had to get back for school.

Fast-forward many years. The couple realized that God knows everyone by name, even while in the mother's womb. The couple had never named the child they lost. They didn't know if it was a boy or girl. They chose the name Eerin. It was different and would work for either a boy or a girl.

Skip forward a few more years. The couple were asleep one night, and the dad had a vision from God. He said it wasn't just a dream; it was a very real feeling. He woke up trembling and couldn't stop. At breakfast, his wife asked what was wrong as he was still trembling. He said he had a vision from God. He said he was in this beautiful place; *beautiful* didn't come close to describing it. He was walking along holding some beautiful young girl's hand. She had long light-brown hair parted down the middle. They both were singing and as happy as they could be. They both stopped and turned to each other. He noticed that the girl had the same kind of nose that his daughter did. She spoke only one word to him: "Daddy." His response was, "Eerin." That's when the vision ended. Now this happened on a Saturday night going on Sunday morning. When they got church, he told his friends and pastor about his vision. He wasn't sure if they believed him or not. But it didn't matter. He knew it was a true vision from God.

Fast-forward a couple years. The kids had all grown up and moved out. The couple went on a weekend trip to visit one of the mom's sisters in a different state. They would get there on Friday and would leave sometime Saturday afternoon for home. While they were there, they all liked to go to antique shops and look around at everything. The husband saw a painting in one of the antique shops. He was shocked by the painting. He went and told his wife about it. She had been in a different part of the store. Her husband said, "You have to see this painting." She went to see it. She said it was a nice painting of a young girl. And the husband said, "You don't understand—that is Eerin. *Our* Eerin."

They didn't buy the painting at that time. They went on home after the day of shopping, but on the way home, the man saw a billboard that said, "Did you get your blessing from God today?" He got to thinking about it, so he called the antique shop to see if they would hold the painting for them; they would be back the next weekend. The next weekend, they went back to the antique shop and got the painting. When they got home, they did some investigating about the painter. He had been a local painter in that area that died in 1956. The painting may have been one of his family members; no one knew who it was. Not much else could be found out about him. The couple found this kind of strange because they both were born in 1956. The painting was painted before they were even one year old. Only God could have known all that was going to happen. He planned it that way. The painting hangs on their bedroom wall, and no matter where you go in the room, the eyes seem to follow you. Sounds kind of strange and maybe a little creepy, but I guess it is a God thing. Let me change that—I *know* that it is a God thing. Only God can give visions and blessings like that. Thank You, Lord.

Visiting Grandsons

There once was a couple, and they still are. They had two grandsons and some granddaughters. Now these two boys were good boys and still are—well, kind of. They're men now. Both of them liked to play football when they were young, or at least they played. They were on the same team: the Back-River Panthers. These two families didn't live in the same town or even the same state, so they would try to get together about once a year or so. It couldn't always happen. You know there was school, jobs, and other stuff that got in the way. But when they did get together, it was a treat for all of them.

Well, it just so happens that every time they got together, there was one thing the boys would ask their grandparents. Not "How are you?" or "How long can you stay?" It was, "Are you going to take us out for ice cream?" This was okay with the grandparents; they didn't mind at all. They actually loved it. It was nice to know that the boys wanted to spend time with them. And still when they get together, the now young men ask, "Are you going to take us out for ice cream?" And the grandparents still love it. Doesn't everyone love doing things together with their family, and who doesn't like ice cream? And what could be better than eating ice cream with family? The grandparents just wish it could have been more often and hope that everyone else did too. That is the getting together part; the ice cream was just a bonus.

What Makes You Cry

All people are made up differently. Here is what I mean. Some people cry when they are scared, sad, mad, lonely, or just having a pity party. Some cry when they are happy or see someone else crying. Crying when someone else cries is what is called being soft-hearted or compassionate. There's nothing wrong with that. There's an old saying, "You would cry at the drop of a hat." Did you know you can cry for several reasons at the same time? Scared, sad, mad, lonely, having a pity party, and happy all at the same time? I would bet you have, but I don't bet. Let's take a closer look.

When a close loved one dies, you might be scared. What will life be without them? They did everything for me. You cry. When a close loved one dies, you might be sad; you will miss them. You cry. When a close loved one dies, you might be mad at them for leaving you. You cry. When a close loved one dies, you might be lonely, just thinking about what you will do without them. You cry. When a close loved one dies, you might have a pity party (that is just totally thinking of no one else except yourself). You cry. When a close loved one dies, you might be happy that they are going to be with Jesus. You cry. That is a time to be happy; you cry happy tears. Your loved one will be with Jesus. They will have no tears, no pain, no crying, no sickness, no worry, no sorrow—no kidding, it is for real. So just make sure when a close loved one dies, you can be happy. It doesn't have to be a close loved one. It could be a neighbor or just someone you know or see somewhere.

The Bible tells us to love one another; that means tell them about Jesus. It doesn't say just a few or the nice ones, or the pretty ones, or the handsome ones, or the ones that smell good, or the tall ones, or the short ones, or the skinny ones, or the heavy ones, or the ones who have a house to live in, not just a cardboard box—you get the idea. Think about it. There are a lot of different kinds of people, but they are all just people, God's creation, the same as you. Where do you want to go when you die? Where will you go when you die? Where do you want your love ones to go when they die? Where do you want the people whom you know to go when they die? Where do you want other people to go?

Remember, Jesus loves everyone. So go ahead and tell everyone about Jesus! He will give you the words to say. The more you do it, the easier it gets. There is a saying, "Don't ask don't tell." That doesn't go for Jesus. Just tell someone! Or you can just sit there and cry a lot.

Yard Ornaments? Pine Noodles?

There once was a little girl who liked to play with Nana's plastic yard animals. They weren't very big animals, only about six inches tall. It was interesting. She would pretend that they were real and could talk. When she and Nana played together, Nana would always have to be the bad, mean animals. I didn't know that bunnies, chipmunks, and squirrels were that mean to one another, or why they were even mean. The animals sometimes made their way into the house, but not on their own, of course. In the house, they liked to hide in the living room under the coffee table. This way, they didn't get kicked or stepped on; they were safely hidden from feet. This was okay, except for when other people came to visit Nana and Papaw. They might have thought it was strange that the animals were in the house, hiding under the coffee table. Maybe the animals were waiting for the weather to change; it could have been too hot or too cold, or too wet or too dry. Or maybe they were there hibernating in the house. But when spring came, they didn't move back outside; it might have been too rainy or hot to go outside. They don't know how long they stayed in the house. And it didn't matter what others thought because the family didn't care; they had fun playing inside with the animals. No matter what time of the year or what the weather was, the animals were welcome in the house. So does that mean they are house ornaments, not yard ornaments? Think about it.

And now on to pine noodles. How do you explain to your cute little granddaughter that they are pine needles, not pine noodles? She has called them noodles for several years now. I have even caught myself calling them noodles and not needles even when she is not around.

Young Lives

There once was a young girl with blonde hair and green eyes. She had a girlfriend named Cindy, whom she spent the night with sometimes. One weekend when she was at Cindy's house, there was a knock at the door. It was a young man who had very curly hair. It was Cindy's cousin; his name was Donald. He had just gotten his first car; it was a station wagon. He wanted to take his cousin for a ride. She said she couldn't go; she had a friend over. Donald said the friend could come along too; he didn't care. But the young girl had to call home to see if it would be okay. Her parents said it was okay since it would be the three of them, so they all went for a ride.

Several days later, Donald asked Cindy to set up a time for the three of them to get together again. She did. He wanted to see the green-eyed girl again. That was when and how they started dating. On the first date, he asked her to marry him. That was fast! It wasn't till the fourth date that she said yes. They had to wait until they both had graduated from high school. That was a couple years down the road. Donald was to graduate a year before his green-eyed girl, Paula. Paula graduated early; she graduated on the twenty-third. This was in January, not May with the rest of her class. Don and Paula then got married on the twenty-fifth of January. Everything was planned. Paula even had made her dress in one of her classes. And that is how their lives together started.

About the Author

Paula Gilliland is a Christian homemaker in Clarksville, Tennessee, who grew up in the little town of Tell City, Indiana, where she met her childhood sweetheart in high school. She had the dream of one day being a wife and mother and fulfilled those dreams soon after graduating from high school. Paula spent a lot of her life on the go with her family after her husband joined the military. After twenty years, they made their home in Clarksville.

She is a great seamstress and cook and loves to be outdoors watching the wonders of life, particularly the butterflies.

She lives for serving God at their church and loves teaching the little children and, of course, working in the kitchen. She always lives with the idea of being the change you want to see in the world. Her life verse from Scriptures is Philippians 4:4: "Rejoice in the Lord always and again I say rejoice."